so you're having an existential crisis

an existential crisis

a roadmap for lost souls

A Pursuit of Wonder publication.
Published by Pursuit of Wonder, 2025.
pursuitofwonder.com

ISBN: 9798283673783

Contents

Introduction – 1

Part 1: Finding Oneself

Chapter 1   Who We Are – 13

Chapter 2   Body – 19

Chapter 3   Mind – 22

Chapter 4   Personality – 27

Chapter 5   Humanity – 30

Chapter 6   Mortality – 34

Chapter 7   Race – 37

Chapter 8   Gender – 45

Chapter 9   Class – 49

Chapter 10   What's Been Done to You – 55

Part 2: Making Oneself

Chapter 11   Sincerity – 61

Chapter 12   Authenticity – 64

Chapter 13   E-Authenticity – 73

Chapter 14   Profilicity – 76

Chapter 15   The Identity Crisis – 78

Chapter 16   Genuine Pretending – 81

Part 3: Becoming Oneself

Chapter 17   Our Ultimate Goal – 91

Chapter 18   The Vital Lie of Character – 95

Chapter 19   The Dizziness of Freedom – 98

Chapter 20   Free Will – 101

Chapter 21   The Myth of Self-Improvement – 108

Chapter 22   The Will to Survive – 111

Chapter 23   Flow – 115

Chapter 24   Self-Complexity – 120

Chapter 25   The Will to Power – 124

Chapter 26   The Autotelic Personality – 128

Part 4: Being Yourself

Chapter 27   Desire – 139

Chapter 28   Alienation – 144

Chapter 29   Love – 147

Chapter 30   Happiness – 153

Chapter 31   The Absurd – 155

Afterword – 171

Acknowledgments – 177

Bibliography – 179

About the Author – 191

Introduction

The unexamined life is not worth living.

—Socrates

Why do a certain number of people, across varying social contexts and time periods, subject themselves to endless analysis and speculation? For Socrates, it was because such a life dedicated to the love of wisdom is, by all accounts, a worthy one. But why?

I remember struggling with this argument when I first cracked open a philosophy book in my mid-teens. At the time, I believed that Socrates was simply imploring us to spend our time poring over stuffy books with furrowed brows. From this perspective, the philosophical life seemed to be pretty depressing and boring. This is somehow *a good life*? I wanted to live! To travel and meet new people and experience the wonders of our world. An existence dedicated to the study of metaphysical principles and debates over transcendental idealism seemed to me like a severe waste of time.

Deep down, I believed that life was simple. Become successful, be likable, and have a family. Check these boxes, and you are guaranteed happiness. Why overthink it? Philosophy was, in my opinion, for the vapid and the pretentious—those who were scared of truly engaging with the realities of the world.

Of course, like many, my teens and early twenties were characterized by a severe identity crisis that would throw my notion of life deeply into question. Seemingly unquestionable truths that I held about the world were shaken up. And many of my basic aims in life suddenly appeared far less clearly defined and further out of my reach than I had previously assumed.

What is success? Why are some people happy without a family? And why was anyone doing anything at all if these answers appeared to be so unclear? My neat and tidy view of the world collapsed. Good things happen to bad people, and bad things happen to good people. Sometimes, you can work hard, and it will not pay off. Without warning, loved ones can pass away. Who would choose such an existence—a life lived entirely at the whim of capriciousness? I had just as much trouble understanding who I was as I did in comprehending what I should do with the rest of my life. My past seemed to have been entirely out of my control. Which school I had been transferred to. Which neighborhood I had grown up in. Were all of my friendships simply based on proximity? I came to view my life as primarily composed of things I had little say in. It was not a life I chose but rather one that was formed largely through contingency.

Another issue emerged. *What should I do with my life?* There are so many options to choose from, and yet there isn't a clear sense of which choices are *better* or more worth pursuing when compared with others. Should I go to university, and if so, which one? What do I study? Where will I live? How should I behave at parties? I felt like a thick shell had formed around me; that I had been forced to become this specific person named Ben. And even worse, I had been given no clear direction in which to continue along a journey I had never asked for.

My crisis culminated shortly before a school trip to Europe when I was fifteen. I was depressed, despondent, and overthinking pretty much everything. This school trip would change all of that.

Europe, in many ways, has suffered a considerable history of existential woe. The French Revolution. The Spanish Civil War. The rise of the German Reich.

Unlike my country of Canada, which is fairly young relative to the rest of the world, Europe has a deep and complex history that is riddled with victories and tragedies. What struck me initially was the extent to which Europe embraced and preserved *what had been done*. The Arc de Triomphe. The Colosseum. The remnants of the Berlin Wall. The architecture and memorials of Europe stand as a testament to the endless twists and turns that have shaped the present character of Europe.

Another aspect of European culture that stuck with me was the lively social and political atmosphere. Protests regularly disrupted our daily plans. And curious strangers would enter into debates with my classmates over a wide variety of topics, from the existence of God to the notion of freedom. There was an ambient vitality that resonated throughout cafés and tapas bars that I could only describe as the buzzing of humanity itself. The world felt awake and refreshingly alive. And for the first time in months, as I walked the cobblestone streets of Paris and plunged into the icy waters of San Sebastien, I, too, felt alive.

What was at the root of this evident spirit in the air? I learned, through our tour guide, that the French education system generally requires the teaching of philosophy at an early age. He explained that French culture is quite conversational, although this could appear confrontational for those less accustomed. Philosophizing was the national sport.

Now, for me, growing up in a culture that championed the pursuit of material wealth as well as emotional inhibition, I found the very thought of "wasting" one's time learning about philosophy and then willingly subjecting oneself to heated debates to be entirely absurd. Philosophy led to no measurable outcome. Philosophy was far too removed from the realities of everyday life. But these beliefs, informed by the society I had grown up in, weakened with every espresso and chance encounter at a Monet. The more I reflected, the more I came around to the possibility that Socrates was right. I had experienced firsthand the vitality of European life. And from what I had gathered, this was a life that was naturally and fervently examined. It was a far more *philosophical* life than what I had been exposed to in North America. And, well, I couldn't bring Europe back with me, so I decided to set a small personal goal for myself that would (I hoped) maintain a little bit of that magic I had felt across the pond: *I would examine my life*. And what was the worthy tool at my disposal? *Philosophy*.

At the age of fifteen, I cracked open my father's copy of *The Outsider* (also often translated as *The Stranger*) by Albert Camus. The novel, which can be read in an evening, is told through the perspective of Meursault, a man who appears to show little remorse over the death of his mother. Meursault horrified me. His actions and behavior appeared so misaligned with the world around him. He is written as an entirely amoral character—someone who does not see things in terms of good or bad. Rather, his style of living is entirely psychologically detached and indifferent. He does things simply because there is nothing else to do. Even when he murders a complete stranger, there is little motivation beyond the intense glare of sunlight. Meursault appeared so alien to my fifteen-year-old self—who had gone through great pains in order to understand the world around me and make the "correct" decisions in life. How could a character treat life so arbitrarily? Reading *The Outsider* disturbed me tremendously. And it also confused me.

What was Albert Camus trying to say? And who was Camus? I was beginning to get the first taste of what it is like to live philosophical-ly—the hunger that drives one to answer *why* beyond all else. I felt like a detective trying to solve the mystery of why this book existed and, just as importantly, why it had affected me so tremendously.

I learned that Camus had also written a philosophical essay, "The Myth of Sisyphus," which could be used as an explanatory guide to *The Outsider*. Skimming through the pages was an intimidating task. Every sentence was jam-packed with obscure names and references. Husserl. Dostoevsky. Nietzsche. Regardless of my relative ignorance of the subject, I nonetheless pledged to myself that I would try to finish "The Myth of Sisyphus" even if I failed to understand a single idea. Perhaps this motivation was driven by the sentence that began Camus's essay, an idea that perfectly illustrated the crisis that had enveloped my existence until that point: "There is only one really serious philosophical problem, and that is suicide."

Despite my experience in Europe, I still held tightly to the idea that philosophy is far from a practical venture. It is for thinking and not for doing. But here, Camus places the very question of how one is to live at the center of philosophy itself. Namely, why should we continue living if so much of the human condition is plagued by meaninglessness? If I wish to do anything practical, I would first need to determine what is worth doing. This is, in a sense, the most practical question out there! For Camus, the purpose of philosophy is to sincerely inquire into this problem. Only through honest and deliberate reflection could we reach some sort of conclusion as to what constitutes a life worth living in the face of meaninglessness and the threat of nihilism.

As I read those words, I felt a strong and intimate camaraderie with a man who had passed away decades ago in a country far from my home. I felt seen and understood. This was the magic of philosophy! The ability for us to share our subjective experience as a common project, through language and reflection. It was as if I were entering into a centuries-long conversation between thinkers of various backgrounds who had all deeply considered the same topics. This experience I had been going through was one that Camus, among many other philosophers, writers, and artists, had also once felt. In fact, I came to realize that it was something undergone by pretty much anyone who had, at one point in time, stared into the vast expanse of a starry night and questioned the point of it all. Philosophy clarified the central issue of my life at the time. By diving into Sartre, Camus, Nietzsche, Marcel, Jung, Kierkegaard, Beauvoir, and many others, I was able to confidently label what had been happening to me. I was having an *existential crisis.* But what is such a crisis?

> Imagine a happy group of morons who are engaged in work. They are carrying bricks in an open field. As soon as they have stacked all the

bricks at one end of the field, they proceed to transport them to the opposite end. This continues without stop, and every day of every year they are busy doing the same thing. One day one of the morons stops long enough to ask himself what he is doing. He wonders what purpose there is in carrying the bricks. And from that instant on he is not quite as content with his occupation as he had been before. I am the moron who wonders why he is carrying the bricks!

Irvin Yalom spent his life formulating a therapy that could treat our existential woes. The passage above comes from a letter written by one of his patients—one of many who were afflicted by what Yalom calls the *ultimate concerns* of existence: death, freedom, isolation, and meaninglessness. I find that this excerpt captures especially well the sort of isolation that could be felt when one steps back and takes a look at their circumstances—especially with the use of the term *moron*. You can feel like nothing is comprehensible, as if everything has been put into question.

An existential crisis is an impasse, a deadlock where the unfolding of the self has been bound by a persistent and gnawing disconcertment. The urge to philosophize could grow quite strong. And here, I would argue, one of the first steps in adequately philosophizing is to be found within the embrace of idiocy. Yes, it is quite humbling. To understand that we actually know very little. An existential crisis is a poignant reminder of this fact. We come to learn that we barely even have a strong grasp of who we are, of what we are doing with our lives, and whether any of this is worth it in the end. Human existence, when viewed through the lens of someone who is existentially anguished, could be considered as quite moronic.

But this is something that *should* be embraced. When I opened up Camus's *The Myth of Sisyphus and Other Essays*, I had to accept the fact that I struggled to comprehend many of the names and a majority of the ideas that he would present. I had to embrace the fact that I was going to feel like an idiot. To truly philosophize, one must be an idiot. This is the task of the philosopher, according to Gilles Deleuze. He writes, "The philosopher takes the side of the idiot as though of a man without presuppositions." The idiot is the subject of the philosopher—a role played by Dionysus and Socrates in the respective works of Nietzsche and Plato. As idiots, the philosopher turns over every rock, examines every inconsistency, and is never *too* comfortable. They pursue truth above all else, and that means they must refuse any givens or any appeals to common sense. And yes, perhaps this will be an exercise in futility. The philosopher may even end up more disillusioned and hopeless than they once were. But once you see a world *divested of light and illusion*, it's quite hard to return to that place of comfortable naivete. The honorable act, in the mind of the philosopher, is to go forward and explore the unknown.

This book is the product of a decade's worth of existential befuddlement. It is an attempt to synthesize all of the ideas I came across as I sought to answer these philosophical mysteries. In other words, it is the outcome of my sincere lifelong pledge towards idiocy—the basic acknowledgment that I know very little. As a result, I have been compelled to lead a life of vigorous curiosity and exploration. To insatiably pursue any and all opportunities that could answer the general question of *why.*

Why do I get out of bed in the morning? Why do we fall in love? Why was I compelled to pick up this book and not that one? And why do anything at all if we are going to die? Not only has the attempt to answer these *whys* amounted to reading and engaging with a wide variety of thinkers and theories that will be presented throughout this book, but it has also led to a life in which I have earnestly and fervently applied these ideas. Ever since I took on the Socratic task of examining my existence, I have entered into a journey that I could have never imagined at the age of fifteen.

I learned that, at the end of the day, Socrates was correct. An unexamined life is not worth living. And, just as importantly, I came to understand that Socrates was not simply advising us to stay inside and navel gaze. To truly examine your life does not mean that you should resign your existence to quiet and academic contemplation. *First and foremost, you need a life to actually examine!* I would argue that to live philosophically means to live fully and earnestly. It involves a tacit commitment to growth and satiating one's curiosity. It necessitates, above all, applying and experimenting with certain philosophical concepts and then reflecting on their general correspondence with reality.

With this in mind, I have maintained my adolescent goal of living a life filled with travel and socializing and have found that a philosophical life is one spent with just as much doing as thinking and reflecting. My curiosity for both philosophy and film culminated in a YouTube channel that is presently sitting at one million subscribers. My interest in the human condition has led me into the world of psychology, where I have been able to publish research on eudaemonia and pursue a PhD in clinical psychology. And on a less quantifiable scale, this journey has brought me to strange places and in conversation with interesting people.

I have been fortunate enough to backpack across Patagonia, volunteer at a giant tortoise breeding center in the Galapagos Islands, coach a youth basketball team, and take in the wonderful collections of MOMA and the Met. I have also been privileged to interview a host of interesting figures, from escaped cult members to fellow content creators, as well as politicians such as Marianne Williamson and academics such as Richard Wolff and John Vervaeke. These experiences have forced me to grow and challenge many of my own preconceptions. Good or bad, they have offered me the opportunity to understand myself and the world around me. And yes, this journey has equally been defined by a great deal of hardships, mental health issues, periods of isolation, and serious self-doubt. Breakups. Regrets. Addiction. To live means to put oneself out there, and this always involves some risk of harm or, at the very least, discomfort. It has not always been so easy or fun. But I would say, with confidence, that it has been entirely worth living.

The following chapters tackle the issues of identity, freedom, desire, and mortality that tend to characterize an existential crisis. Beginning with one of the fundamental questions—*Who am I?*—we will then move the conversation towards the question of *Who could I become?* These first two parts largely revolve around the concept of identity and freedom; namely, how stable and "real" is the self? What is it composed of? Can it be altered? And how much freedom do we have in this alteration or process of becoming?

The final two sections attempt to answer what one is to do when faced with such an existential dilemma. What is worth pursuing? What is desire? And can we be happy while maintaining a lucid awareness of our condition as a mortal and conscious creature? The first two parts of the book deal with the contingency of our existence—*what has been done to us.* Aspects of our identity such as race and gender as well as the very means of identity-making require sufficient examination for self-understanding. Parts 3 and 4 then look towards the future, asking: *What can we do with what has been done to us? Are we capable of change? And what exactly should we change about ourselves, if anything?*

The answers may not always be satisfactory. The thinkers that have so profoundly influenced my own journey may nonetheless fall flat for you. And I would underscore here that this book represents a very small sample of the total sum of writers, philosophers, poets, artists, and many other talented individuals who have spent their lives in an attempt to answer these questions. My placement as an English-speaking Canadian biases me towards the Western canon, although we will drift eastward in the latter parts of the book. Nonetheless, I hope this extensive overview of how one could live a worthy existence encourages you to engage in your own journey of self-examination and growth. At the very least, I hope that my words can offer that respite from the isolation I felt when reading Camus as a teenager—a moment between us, two humans struggling along in the dark, lodged in a precarious situation, trying our best.

Part 1

Finding Oneself

Chapter 1

Who We Are

In this part, we begin our investigation into the existential crisis by exploring "what" we are. This involves a brief overview of what it means to exist. Who are we? And, on a similar note, are those aspects that comprise us actually worthy to hold on to? A discussion of identity as it relates to class, gender, personality, and race follows.

The first thing that might come up when you are wading through existentially murky waters is the question of identity. Who are you? After all, we primarily experience everything through ourselves (and not our friend Todd or our cat Hubert). To experience some confusion over who we are, then, is to problematize our existence. How we relate to the world could feel completely knocked off course. And this sensation can invariably hold hands with that grim reaper of mental health: *depression*. Psychiatrist Alain Ehrenberg describes this experience quite well, stating:

> Depression reminds us in no uncertain terms that to be the owner of oneself does not mean that everything is possible—all that rises and falls within us, that contracts and expands. Because it stops us, depression holds our attention: it reminds us that we have not left the human realm and that the latter remains chained to a system of meanings that simultaneously go beyond it and constitute it.

Yes, depression is a miserable state of mental anguish. But we can also recognize it as an opportunity for greater self-understanding.

Depression forces us to stop and look around at who we are. And if we eventually shake off those heavy shackles of sleep-ins, mood swings, and anhedonia, perhaps we can even discover who we might become. In the end, all we can wish for is some self-acceptance in terms of what that is—to find contentment in being through becoming. But first, let us take on the task of discovering *who we are.*

The Dual Model of the Existential Crisis

For whatever rhyme or reason, you have ended up in this body, with this name, and these attributes. It all seems so…arbitrary.

But is it really arbitrary? Arbitrariness tends to signify a sort of limitless freedom. I can make some coffee. I can dance in the streets. I can marry this person or that person. Most of these choices may feel fairly arbitrary in the grand scheme of things. That is, they hold little weight on a vast cosmic scale. But what about all of those elements that occurred before we could make a choice? Although we may have some freedom in terms of what we choose to do, what about those variables of our existence that have been chosen for us?

This is the difference between *arbitrariness* and *contingency.* Whereas something is arbitrary because the choices are seemingly limitless, contingency points to the lack of options we have available to us. We might feel like we have several options in terms of how we spend our day. But yesterday—the day that we have already spent—cannot be changed. Yesterday, you may have planned to go to the movies. But then you started coughing and decided to stay home instead. Because of this, you were finally able to call your mother. Then, while on the phone, your mother mentioned a great recipe for chicken pot pie, and so you spent the remainder of the day cooking.

While there was certainly some freedom involved in how you went about your day, much of it was evidently informed by things outside of your control. In other words, much of what we do is already molded by what has been done to us.

On a larger scale, we could just as easily have been born to other parents in a different country, at a different time. We like to think that our lives are dictated by rationally determined choices we make, but upon some reflection, we realize that we may have only chosen to move for university or change careers out of some chance encounter or moment of contingency.

The existentialist Martin Heidegger had a perfect word for such contingency—*thrownness* (or *Geworfenheit*). We are thrown into the world without consent, and we inherit an arbitrary set of traits that characterize our identity and the direction of our lives. Born to a rich family in 1950s California? You'll be thrown in the direction of fame and fortune. Born with the same amount of wealth during Mao's Great Cultural Revolution? Things might turn out differently. From our vantage point, there's very little rhyme or reason as to why we are thrown into the world as *this* instead of *that*—man or woman, Black or White, blind or paraplegic. This is to say that our existence is likely built on contingent foundations.

However, this is *not* an argument that equates contingency with determinism. Instead, existentialists such as Heidegger regularly endorsed the utilization of one's freedom. Although much of who we are and what has been done to us has shaped our present circumstances, it does not follow that we are condemned to follow the trajectory of our pasts. Being born rich does not guarantee a certain existence, although certain odds are heightened, and others are lowered.

Despite our thrownness, we are still more free than we care to admit. One of the most inspiring examples of human liberty is represented in the work of Victor Frankl, a psychotherapist who had experienced the inhumane and nightmarish conditions of Nazi[†] concentration camps.

---

† Yes, there is considerable irony in placing Heidegger and Frankl together, with the former being a willing member to the Nazi Party of Germany. Here I take a pragmatic approach in discussing Heidegger (similar to Richard Rorty) and see him both as attached to his historical context and still someone with substantial influence on the existentialist tradition, and thus worth mentioning. Many of these thinkers, sadly, are bad company—misogynists, racists, drunkards, and outright psychos. Let us hope the future generation of philosophers are also better humans.

Although Frankl had been deprived of basic dignity, he nonetheless recognized the power of freedom found in how one reacts to their present circumstances. He writes, "Everything can be taken from a man but one thing: the last of human freedoms—to choose one's attitude in any given set of circumstances, to choose one's own way."

We arguably do have some say in what we end up doing. Nonetheless, many of us accept this thrownness as a given. We tell ourselves that, for whatever reason, we just aren't very good at math and choose not to take a class that, otherwise, we might find to be quite interesting. Unfortunately, many of us resign ourselves to the mantra of the status quo: *It is what it is.* We never question our situation and the way we have been *thrown* into the world. But Heidegger argued that recognizing and examining our thrownness is, paradoxically, a step in the direction of breaking such a cycle. "The thrower of the project is thrown in his own throw. How can we account for this freedom? We cannot. It is simply a fact, not caused or grounded, but the condition of all causation and grounding." A little confusing, no? Perhaps this is better summed up in Jean-Paul Sartre's simple phrase: "Freedom is what you do with what's been done to you."

The contingency of our existence, what has been done to us, is solid and unchangeable. However, within that space, we still have the freedom to react. We still have the chance to change things.

Take yourself, for example. Right now, you read these words, carry some family name, and live in a certain country with its own peculiar geopolitical conditions. You may also have been thrown into a time of war, environmental collapse, and growing inequality. This is your context.

And now, with this awareness and acceptance of your condition, you can choose what to do with what has been done to you. This sort of worldview reflects the principle underlying acceptance and commitment therapy (or ACT), a highly efficacious treatment for anxiety and depression. ACT uses mindfulness techniques, among other interventions, in order to teach patients how to accept, rather than escape or avoid, negative events and feelings. This is so they can approach life with greater clarity and precision, where they can adequately commit to what needs to be done in the present.

Committing, however, is often easier said than done. What is the *correct* thing to commit ourselves to achieving? This second aspect of the existential crisis—the arbitrariness of our decisions—can feel like just as much of a challenge as the overcoming of our own facticity.

Every choice—from what we wear to whom we decide to marry—comes with it the limitation of other opportunities and the possibility that we have judged poorly. The criteria for what is the right choice can change abruptly. We may be brought up religious, only to experience a crisis of faith and, consequently, the need to reassess what actually matters. A life devoid of sin may have been your initial plan. But what is considered sinful can vary considerably. Determining right from wrong becomes almost impossible with no sense of direction. In short, how we choose to live can seem arbitrary in the grand scheme of things. And so the process of overcoming an existential crisis must involve the establishment of some sort of direction—a reliable roadmap on which to base our decisions.

Now, with all that being said, we need to first accept some things about ourselves before we commit to becoming who we want to be. Before we tackle the challenge of arbitrariness, we must first face our present situation in all of its contingencies. Psychologist Alfred Adler emphasized the importance of this with one of his central ideas: *the psychology of use.* Adler thought that people were not solely defined by their supposed traits and features. Rather, they were characterized by how they made use of these more innate qualities. However, to cultivate this sort of responsibility, the individual must first become aware of these traits. In the same manner we would go about initiating any sort of project, we must first become intimately familiar with the tools we will be using. The project of becoming who we are, then, must be accompanied by an initial stage in which we attend to our tools, those seemingly stable aspects of identity that we have inherited through contingency.

This journey of self-discovery is a difficult process. To help us understand it better, this first section is intentionally focused on the sort of contingency we may feel when we look back at our lives and who we are. We may experience some resentment, anger, or despair. What can be changed?

Under the principles of ACT, it is perhaps best to explore these elements of contingency with clarity and precision. In other words, we have to first understand what exactly has been done to us. Who are we right now? What tools or equipment are we working with? *Who* have we been thrown into? In seeking these answers, we may find ourselves better able to determine which aspects of our lives are alterable and, on the other hand, which parts of ourselves are more fixed.

The following pages will take us on a journey through all of those things that inform our identity. It is important to remember that an existential crisis, more often than not, is a sign that one or perhaps several elements of our identity have been disturbed. And so, in this journey, we will also take time to explore when these supposedly stable aspects of identity can destabilize and send us into a crisis. In keeping with Sartre's notion that freedom is what you do with what's been done to you, let us look first at what has been done to us. Strap in!

Chapter 2

Body

Life's most direct path to achieving its own maintenance is by following
the dictates of homeostasis, the intricate set of regulatory procedures that
made life possible when it first bloomed in early single-cell organisms.

— Antonio Damasio, *Feeling and Knowing*

Ghrelin, dopamine, and the irritating buildup of lactic acid. Even the
goosebumps you experience when outside on a wintery day are all
processes that are in the service of maintaining this meat cage that is
you. The endocrine system and central nervous system all collaborate
tirelessly just for you to get by—an impressive operation that lasts some
sixty to eighty years for most. Isn't there something amazing about how
all of this can happen with no real conscious input? This is your body,
the first stop in our journey through who we are.

Our body is a miracle in terms of biological efficiency. But isn't there
also something somewhat terrifying about this mass of flesh and bone?
The sagging, the wrinkles, the easy ways in which it can fail us? Franz
Kafka, in his work *The Metamorphosis*, brilliantly captures the sort of
grotesque sense of alienation we may feel in our own bodies. In Kafka's
story, Gregor Samsa awakens one day as a giant disgusting bug and,
unable to communicate with his family, must contend with the decisions
of those around him. What is interesting about Gregor's predicament
isn't so much that he is horrified or confused as to how exactly he ended
up as a giant bug (in fact, he accepts it quite quickly). Rather, it's in the
burden he feels towards his family and in his inability to take on the tasks

of everyday life that most fill his mind with worries and anxieties. This burden is entirely rooted in his relationship with his own body, a cumbersome and grotesque unit of biological drives and desires. He can no longer talk. He must crawl on the ground. He scavenges for garbage. He can no longer function as a human being in a human body. His identity is now greatly defined by the contingency of his physical form—an insect.

Throughout the novella, Gregor fails to be properly understood by others. His closest loved ones struggle in their attempts to live with him, shaken by the physical transformation he has so absurdly endured. Gregor is suddenly dehumanized by his loved ones and finds himself almost entirely defined by his physical form. His circumstances represent something that can happen to all of us—the sudden and unpredictable alienation we may experience with our physical selves. Gregor's feelings, a sense of dislocation with himself that emerges from being treated as nothing more than his body, reflects the existential feeling of being defined primarily by our outward appearance. Depending on your interpretation, Gregor's situation could reflect Sartre's famous quote, "Hell is other people."

There is a peculiar horror in being seen as nothing more than one's physicality. To be stripped down to our bare flesh and bones, defined by this clumsy assessment, feels like some sort of existential punishment. How could my outer appearance reflect my inner reality—the complexity and potential of all that I am? This is the sort of hell that Sartre speaks of. Others define us on their terms, and we have little say in the matter. We are condemned to the hell of the other's opinion—minimized and defined by the Other.[†]

Until we become closer with others, this opinion that strangers hold

---

† Why capitalize the O? While several strands of philosophy engage with the idea of the Other, the use of the term *Other* is often invoked in reference to Hegel's idea of the self, not as self-constituting but as being constituted by "others." We are conscious of ourselves because of the existence of a self that we are not. This self that we are not, a general non-self with its own consciousness and self-consciousness, is the Other. According to Hegel, we develop our own sense of self through the presence, affirmation, awareness, and relationship with this Other. The Other, then, is a fundamental component of our own sense of who we are.

over us is more often than not initially formed through their judgment of our outward appearance and behavior. Sadly, several studies demonstrate that we tend to make up our minds about other people in a matter of seconds. This is a somewhat depressing fact. You may be a Nobel Prize winner, an esteemed aristocrat, or a polyglot. But if the first impression that a stranger has of you is accompanied by a terrible haircut or a concerningly large zit, then the chances that they will truly see you for all that you are is slim. Our outward appearance unfortunately comprises a considerable amount of how we are seen and treated.

So what is this special aspect of ourselves that is being dehumanized when we find ourselves in the hell of others' opinions? What are we, outside of our bodies? While he is able to maintain the love he has for his family, a sense of personal identity, and his own peculiar personality, Gregor nonetheless must service a body that is insectoid rather than human. His goals, his actions, and how he relates to the outside world are all fundamentally different from the owner of a human body.

Similarly, we may feel at times restricted by our bodily limitations. We are both capable of imagining entire universes, creating beautiful pieces of art and abstract thinking while, simultaneously, eating, defecating, and fornicating like any other member of the animal kingdom. We possess both seemingly higher and lower qualities. As Nietzsche describes us, we are somewhere between a god and an ape. "In man, creature and creator are united: in man there is matter, fragment, excess, clay, mud, madness, chaos; but in man there is also creator, sculptor, the hardness of the hammer, the divine spectator and the seventh day—do you understand this antithesis?"

Yes, the body certainly informs our existence whether we like it or not. And so who we are is fundamentally embodied in the construct of a specific species—that often has two legs, two arms, and ten fingers. There is an inseparability there—between the body and what we may call the mind. But what is this mind—the creator, the sculptor, the divine spectator? More specifically, what is consciousness?

Chapter 3

Mind

To continue on our theme of homeostasis, the neuroscientist Antonio Damasio views consciousness as a continuation of the purpose of life. Around three and a half billion years ago, when multicellular organisms emerged, things became increasingly more complex. We needed a better system to coordinate all of these little doohickies and hoo-has that regulate our relationship with the environment. This newly evolved system was what we now know as the central nervous system. The nervous system, being the overachiever that it is, went far beyond managing the simple actions of survival. It also began to represent patterns.

This upgrade made managing the tasks of life far more efficient. Now, we could even predict possibly harmful events and prepare for them far before they ever happen! While the anxiety-ridden among us might argue that this is less of a benefit than it is a burden, the gift of consciousness should not be taken for granted. Foresight and imagination are crucial in the process of survival.

One of the more impressive aspects of consciousness is that it appears to be entirely aware of itself! Consciousness can ponder and prod over its own use, its own function, and how it relates to the world at large. This may be one of the benefits of having an existential crisis—we may experience brief moments of awe in the face of newfound truths. An existential crisis, in some respects, is simply our mind needing to take some sort of audit. And think about it this way. The matter that existed in the universe for trillions of years gathered itself in such a way and arranged its environment in such a way that it can now understand the very words being read about itself! The mind has allowed for perhaps one of the few worthwhile gifts known to life: *the capacity for the universe to know itself.*

How, then, do the mind and body interact? While different schools of thought have bickered endlessly over the extent to which the mind and body are connected (or are even one and the same), it is reasonable to presume that the mind is inseparably related to the physical world. In other words, consciousness relies on at least some physical elements in order to emerge. At the very least, it needs neurons, cortices, and all of the lower-body functions that maintain it in order to actually be aware of the world around itself. And it also needs something to be conscious of, right? Try to imagine nothingness. Try your best to visualize what it was like to be you before you were born. Difficult, right? Our consciousness is evidently embodied and relies on the physical world for its existence.

Thinkers such as Henri Bergson and Heidegger have greatly emphasized this embodied role of consciousness. This is best presented in the field of phenomenology, a precursor to existentialism. Unlike theories of the mind that see consciousness as a sort of "ghost in the machine"—where the mind and body appear distinct and separate—phenomenology views subjectivity (our inner experience) as fundamentally emerging from a relationship between the world and ourselves. We do need to rely on the outside world to reliably understand ourselves, and this is presumably done through the interaction between consciousness and the environment.

The embodied self—as described by the suave existentialist Maurice Merleau-Ponty—is the phenomenological concept of selfhood that champions this corporeal and sensory interaction as the core of our subjectivity. Yes, we find ourselves aware of ourselves and thrown into particular physical circumstances. But Merleau-Ponty makes it clear that this extends beyond interactions with physical objects. Intercorporeality—the clash and cohesion of other bodies with our own—likewise informs our phenomenology of the self. And through this, a sense of self develops. We find ourselves. Notably, the idea of the embodied self opposes the notion of an abstract agent of consciousness. Instead, much like Heidegger, Merleau-Ponty posits that the self is inseparably related to the immediate environment as well as its own physical form.

An effective method to reveal this sort of embodied nature of consciousness is through something that phenomenologists call *bracketing*. Bracketing is the observation and awareness of something without judgment or opinion. To bracket is to look at something like an apple, for example, and withhold any sort of prior knowledge, experience, or memories associated with it. Phenomenologists would use bracketing to describe objects and experiences in strange new ways that stripped them from any presumptions or biases (at least in theory). Thinkers such as Husserl would spend hours practicing this in order to lay bare the structure of consciousness.

Take, for example, the experience of eating Cool Ranch Doritos. Really pay attention here. Notice that when you experience the saltiness and the subsequent cooling effect on your taste buds, it is as if you cease to be you. You are your taste buds. You are the saltiness. You find yourself being interconnected with the world and its contents. You simply are whatever you are conscious of at that moment in time. Sartre puts it far more succinctly than I ever could:

> If impossibly you were to enter a consciousness, you would be picked up by a whirlwind and thrown back outside to where the tree is and all the dust, for consciousness has no inside. It is merely the exterior of itself and it is this absolute flight, this refusal to be substance, that constitutes it as consciousness.

What the phenomenologists discovered was something that Eastern traditions have been describing for centuries. Bracketing leads to a sort of collapse of selfhood—the dissolution of the ego. We come to understand that we are what we decide to direct our awareness towards. This is perhaps best articulated by Jiddu Krishnamurti—an avid practitioner of looking at things as they are. Rather than viewing intelligence as something that could be measured in terms of efficiency, IQ scores, or the amount of knowledge someone has, Krishnamurti instead argued that intelligence mainly comes from awareness without judgment. This can be attained through cultivating the art of seeing— something that we might nowadays call mindfulness. In one discussion with a listener, Krishnamurti urges them to *truly* see a mountain range. To actually observe it with no assumptions, preconceptions, or (most importantly) effort. When one uses effort to observe, then they are already looking beyond what they see. The task of truly seeing things should be effortless. As he asks the listener:

> Can the consciousness be empty of all this content? First see the beauty of it, Sir…Because it must empty itself without an effort. The moment there is an effort, there is the observer who is making the effort to change the content, which is part of consciousness.

Through this sort of observation, we find ourselves to be nothing more than the content of our observation. Right now, close your eyes and pay attention to your breath. After some time, as your heart rate lowers, ask yourself to wait for your next thought. Do not think about what sort of thoughts will appear. Just wait, patiently. What occurs in this space between waiting and that first thought? I would presume some sense of non-selfhood—an absence of identity and ego. This sort of practice reveals the extent to which our consciousness constructs our sense of identity—as well as the ease with which we can pull back and experience the emptiness within.

However, I would also assume that you aren't currently in a monastery, separated from human existence, and thus able to regularly dip into this sort of ego dissolution. As Heidegger proposed, we are thrown into the world as a Dasein, a being-in-the-world, and this world will define you whether you like it or not. All of those contingent elements that make up our identities are ripe for observation, judgment, and even ridicule. We are constantly reminded of our own selfhood through the existence of others. Remember! *Hell is other people.* It is unlikely that most of us could properly navigate modern society under a sense of total ego death. Sartre suggested that because we are inextricably linked to the perception of others, we will always be motivated back towards our ego. The consciousness of others can then influence our very own self-consciousness.

How do others define us? Rather than simply being, we find ourselves regularly defined by two major properties: *what we have* and *what we do*. Because others do not have access to our inner world, they can really only judge us based on our actions and possessions. Unfortunately, this can then inform our own self-perception. This issue has been taken up by many philosophers before—namely, how does society entrap this magical gift that is our consciousness and force us into rigid identities? The existentialist Gabriel Marcel defines the process as *crispation*—we attach who we are to certain possessions and attributes, and so our lives gradually become less about being and more about doing and having. Over time, we mistake who we are for these things as daily habits, and the opinions of others come to occupy our awareness entirely. With this, an outer ontological shell forms around us, and we become rigid in how we see ourselves and life. Our consciousness and what we choose to pay attention to is now constrained. Marcel sees this, understandably, as a tragedy. Human existence should not be seen as some sort of abstract problem that must be fixed by rigidly defining ourselves. Rather, consciousness—*being*—is a mystery that is to be endured and experienced.

Chapter 4

Personality

While we will return to Marcel's inspiring notion of being as mystery, I think it's important to stop here and really consider crispation. How do we come to form this shell around how we choose to define ourselves?

One way to look at this is through our personality—the style in which we express ourselves and act out social behaviors. Each of us has a particular style of expression that is necessary for existing with other conscious creatures. We live, for better or worse, in a social arena. Not only do we have to fare with our lumbering bodies (i.e., intercorporeality) and intricate consciousness, we also have to contend with the fact that we have been thrown into the world with others. To a certain degree, we need to learn how to manage the expectations and opinions of others. What a burden! This is what Sartre meant when he wrote that "Hell is other people"—the burden of being seen by others can be a scenario of unimaginable horror.

We have little control over how people see us and, more often than not, they tend to see us quite differently from how we see ourselves. One ill-timed outburst could give the unfortunate impression that you are mean-spirited, if not downright rude. While you could make some amends in attempting to adjust the opinions of others, it will become readily apparent that others tend to strongly hold on to their opinions. Nietzsche articulates this social misfortune quite clearly: "When we have to change our mind about a person, we hold the inconvenience he causes us very much against him." How we are seen is often out of our control.

So how are we seen exactly? It is thought that from around age two, we go from seeing ourselves in terms of "I" (a self-indulgent *knower* of the world) to seeing ourselves as "Me" (someone who is also being measured and assessed by those around us). We become aware of the need to regulate and monitor our behavior in order to function socially. And how we do this can vary considerably. Personality psychology is a somewhat reliable tool in determining and even predicting how the individual may act in the social world. And *act* is a crucial word here. The sociologist Erving Goffman viewed human social behavior as a performance, much like a theater play. We are actors who go through certain routines (a preestablished pattern of action), and these routines manage the state of ourselves and others in this production we call life.

However, there's always room for improvisation, and we tend to put our own unique twist on our performance. There are so many ways to be a human! And how we study all of these different acting styles is through the subject of personality.

One of the more reliable measures of personality is the Big 5 Personality Index—which is sometimes referred to as the OCEAN traits. This is a helpful mnemonic for remembering the five traits: *openness, conscientiousness, extraversion, agreeableness*, and *neuroticism*. We all vary considerably in the extent to which we express such traits. And each has its own pros and cons. An extroverted individual may seek out social interactions and experience more positive emotionality. However, they may also fail to take negative feedback and use aggression to get their way. Those high on neuroticism are often chronically worried and insecure. However, they can also be quick learners and stay alert in times of danger.

Whatever the case, the important thing to know is that these traits are also (for better or worse) aspects of your identity that you have been thrown into. Personality researcher Dan McAdams writes, "The scientific jury came back about two decades ago. Its verdict was (and remains) that at least half of the variance in personality traits is accounted for by genetic differences between people."

This is thanks to twin studies, where identical twins separated at birth are found to nonetheless express highly similar personalities in terms of the Big 5 model. It has also been concluded that most of these traits remain relatively stable throughout life. An extreme introvert could, for example, develop an appreciation for dinner parties and even cultivate some useful social skills. However, it is unlikely that they will ever become as overly grandiose and bubbly as their more sociable friends. In short, we are at least partially confined to certain limits of personality. Of course personality change is possible—especially in the face of adverse life events—but it would probably do you better to accept some aspects of yourself here.

Chapter 5

Humanity

But you aren't *just* a personality. Animals can have personalities, too! Your dog can be outgoing. Your cat can be reclusive. You're not just thrown into any kind of body or mind. According to most well-respected biologists, you are also thrown into a *human* body and mind.

But what does this mean? Thankfully, you weren't cast into existence as a cow, destined for the slaughter, nor were you born into the fleeting life of the housefly you swatted last week. In a way, you were spared—blessed, even—to be considered a part of this remarkable, brilliant species we call *Homo sapiens.*

Are we that great, though? The topic of speciesism, the idea that we are better than other animals on the basis of being, well, us, was originally presented by Richard Ryder in the 1970s. Peter Singer then expanded on the topic:

> The racist violates the principle of equality by giving greater weight to the interests of members of his own race, when there is a clash between their interests and the interests of those of another race. Similarly, the speciest allows the interests of his own species to override the greater interests of members of other species. The pattern is the same in each case.

Now, are we some equivalent to a racist just because we like eating burgers? As somebody going through an existential crisis, you clearly already have a lot on your plate, so I won't dwell on the ethics of eating meat or the horrors of factory farming. But I think Singer raises an interesting point. Why do we consider ourselves better? I'd gladly put a collar on a cat, but I am much less comfortable with the idea of doing so to one of my friends. That would be demeaning. But why? What do we see in humans that is so special?

I recall a school field trip to the zoo where one of the gorillas came right up to the glass and stared at me. Looking into those dark eyes, I felt a strange uncanniness. On one hand, the creature before me was quite unlike my own species. She was covered in fur, walked mostly with her arms, and possessed a facial structure that one could consider quite alien. And yet I felt a sort of familiarity within her. She was seemingly intelligent in terms of her signaling for food. She also demonstrated some level of emotion—a notable look of curiosity as she stared back through the glass at this hairless, clothed ten-year-old ape. I was struck with a strange feeling. Is who or what we consider to be human on a spectrum? Did this gorilla possess some human qualities—but *not quite enough* qualities to keep her from being placed on display in a cage? Would this make those we consider human—and yet possess some developmental limits in terms of their intelligence and emotional expression—equally deserving of being placed in a zoo? Yes, of course the capability of reproducing within a species is a common benchmark for that which separates us from the chimps and bonobos. But lest we forget, human zoos existed only a century ago. Do we need to point to something solid and grounded in science to justify whether we place one species in a zoo exhibit for the benefit of another? Are zoos of any kind ethical? Where exactly on the spectrum do we become human?

To understand this, it is perhaps best that we elaborate on the idea of humans as being something between a god and an ape. Yes, we are artistic, creative, and spiritual. Many Enlightenment-era thinkers viewed this ability to function as *higher selves*—reasoning machines capable of creativity and morality—as the defining trait when compared to other animals. But are we not also, for better or worse, hairy, hungry, and horny? There may be some limits to our intelligence, ruled by our desires, drives and primal instincts. But it is self-evident that we do seem capable of some fairly complex mental processes and social behavior. Are we, then, marked by this—the fundamental capacity to rise above our more animalistic drives?

Enlightenment thinkers such as Immanuel Kant heralded our capacity for logic and reason as the defining feature of human nature. It is through our drive towards creating a unified theory of reality—a project only achievable through our ability to derive certain truths from our perceptions—that we find what it means to be human.

This is a hotly debated issue. Would individuals incapable or deficient in terms of reasoning not be considered human?[+] I would certainly hope not. And it is not as if, in general, we as a species are brilliant reasoning machines. We often make mistakes and lead ourselves astray through certain biases and heuristics. Nietzsche was quite critical of any such claims on our ability to arrive at fundamental truths through human reason.

Nietzsche, and the existentialists who were inspired by him, asked an important question. What if, rather than being defined by our higher functions, humanness was instead defined by this very tension between what we are and what we could be? Perhaps *rising above* suggests too much in terms of our capabilities. We are, after all, neither paragons of absolute rationality nor dung-flinging primates. As Nietzsche argued, we are somewhere in the middle. Perhaps this precarious position, as some thinkers have proposed, has tragically left us as nothing more than a species that is intelligent enough to understand its own unintelligence. And to face our limitations with such lucidity can be a miserable experience. This is where we may feel the sort of

---

+ This line of reasoning, an extension of the Enlightenment-era philosophers, is still evoked in the service of justifying eugenics and notions of human hierarchy. This is in spite of a relative dearth in evidence that supports any significant differences in cognitive functioning across various categories of humans (i.e., race, gender, nationality).

contingency that marks the existential crisis—the very limits of what it means to be human.

And on a darker note, we appear to be far more aware of our mortality than other organisms. The fact that we can imagine our own deaths at any moment is an unfortunate feature of human consciousness. For some, such as the existential anthropologist Ernest Becker, this awareness is the very marker of our humanity: "Man is literally split in two: he has an awareness of his own splendid uniqueness in that he sticks out of nature with a towering majesty, and yet he goes back into the ground a few feet in order to blindly and dumbly rot and disappear forever."

Although we share a proclivity towards deterioration with the rest of the animal kingdom, it is perhaps here where humans differ most: in the awareness of our own deaths.

Chapter 6

Mortality

Even the most rational among us are still tied to their existence as biological beings. Certainly, we could train ourselves to subjugate our lower desires in pursuit of being pure rational beings. But even then, no matter how successful we are in overcoming our more base characteristics, we will still find ourselves biologically and genetically determined. And nowhere is this more apparent than in the inevitability of our demise. Ernest Becker argues death is perhaps the greatest representation of our weakness as a species. The fact that we can create ideas and worlds that live beyond us is impressive and yet saddening, as these creations still fail to save us from the grave.

For Ernest Becker, this drive to deny death—let alone our own biological limits—forms societies and cultures. For example, Becker views nations as *immortality projects*—large-scale entities we can attach ourselves to that supersede our short time here. Our identity—the character we form as a result of these attachments—is the vessel with which we can use to deny our deaths. If, for example, we were to commit to a religion, this commitment becomes solidified in our identity (and thus becomes a part of us) and "guarantees" that we will live on in some symbolic sense (in an afterlife, for example).

To lay claim to some beliefs and values so fervently, as objects that guarantee your worth and defend you against a meaningless existence, is to strongly suggest that your life choices are capital-T True. The issue is that others will also see their own distinct life choices and identity as true. And, consequently, some may take your own life choices as a threat, as a contradiction that denies them of their own personal truth. According to Becker, this can have some brutal consequences. The basic reality that others pursue different and sometimes contradictory identities (or *character*) to achieve symbolic immortality is of central concern to Becker. He notes that the mere existence of another religion, for example, is an affront to one's own religion and thus directly threatens the whole point of attaching oneself to such an object of symbolic immortality. And so either I'm wrong, or you are. Becker argues that this is a central cause of evil. People have staked their identity on certain immortality projects (nations, ideas, religions) that contradict others. These other projects symbolize the fragility of one's own identity and attachment. This becomes all the more significant when one did not necessarily choose their identity but found themselves born into it. Who you are under these conditions can seem unquestionable. Changing minds just isn't possible. Others are wrong by default.

In a sense, the presence of other identities can represent death itself. Or at the very least, others can represent those more looked-down-upon, creaturely elements of human existence. And in recognizing that the presence of other immortality projects threatens one's own, we see the clash of identities—through the process of physical and emotional violence—as the perpetual cycle of evil that has comprised much of history.

Humans are mortal and fragile to biological constraints. But they can also supersede them by attaching their identities to worthwhile symbolic immortality projects. Arguably, this separates us from animals and thus makes us truly human. To be a human, then, is to possess that *special something*—that symbolic element that can live on past one's biological limits and justify our very being. And so the labeling of another as not human (or less than human) is a claim that the other lacks this special symbolic element.

Now, from a quick glance at some of the worst things we have done to each other, especially when we look at human zoos, the assignment of humanness seems to be of utmost importance, as the capacity to consider someone human or not human tends to inform our treatment of them. This is most apparent in the concept of humanization and dehumanization. As several studies have shown, even relatively progressive individuals may assign varying levels of humanness to other races and ethnicities. This is typically measured through the Ascent of Man measure. This measure asks individuals the extent to which they see a certain group as human and reliably predicts certain attitudes and behaviors that reflect a distrust and active antipathy towards groups considered to be less than human. Research with the measure has found that dehumanization occurs especially in times of threat. For example, in one study, White Americans demonstrated a temporary spike in dehumanization of Arabic people within three days of the Boston Marathon attack. However, these feelings of dehumanization decreased up to six months after the attack, suggesting that dehumanization was influenced by threats to one's in-group.

One of the more harrowing results from these studies is the cycle of dehumanization. If Group A dehumanizes Group B, Group B is more likely to dehumanize Group A. This can quickly result in Group A further dehumanizing Group B, and soon enough, a pernicious cycle develops: *the cycle of dehumanization.* This cycle is characterized by each group hurling increasingly dehumanizing language at one another and even justifying the use of violence. Such a cycle has been hypothesized as one of the driving forces behind some of the worst acts we have committed against each other. Just look at the dehumanizing language used in times of war. The opponent is often seen as a cockroach, a parasite, or some sort of virus. It appears, sadly, that we tend to assign humanness on the basis of living entities that we already identify with.

Chapter 7

Race

The issue of dehumanization is intimately related to the unfortunate persistence of racism. The fact that many groups have been historically treated as less human than others is an unsettling fact. Regardless of one's personality or what they offer to the world, race can nonetheless define how they will be treated. It can fundamentally determine the trajectory of one's life.

And so the issue of race deserves a more thorough analysis. Race is strange. Countless studies demonstrate that, if anything, it's a concept that barely exists—at least on a biological level. For example, one study from Stanford examined the question of race by looking at over 4,000 different alleles (alleles being the different types of genes one could have). If biologically distinct racial groups really existed, researchers would have found trademark alleles and genetic features unique to a single group but not to any other. Instead, they discovered that only 7.4 percent of all alleles were specific to a particular geographical region. This is hardly enough to call such alleles "trademark" alleles. The researchers concluded that there was no evidence that the groups we call Black, Asian, White, or otherwise are genetically distinct.

Aside from a biological basis, our ideas of race are also often defined through ethnicity—the quality of belonging to a particular group of cultural and geographical heritage. The anthropologist Jonathan Rosa highlighted the process that develops as ethnicity comes to inform ideas of race. Specifically, Rosa looked at a high school in Chicago that is primarily attended by Puerto Ricans and Mexicans. His central aim revolved around statements like the following: *I heard that Mexicans are Hispanic, and Puerto Ricans are Latino.* Such statements point to attempts at drawing lines between different identity groups through race. But just how does this process come to be? Rosa found the following:

> Ninth-grade students who had recently entered the school characteristically identified as Puerto Rican or Mexican, but they did not position these identities in rigid opposition to one another. Yet, over the course of students' educational trajectories at New Northwest High School, stereotypes of Mexican-Puerto Rican difference became increasingly important and rigidly defined.

What exactly was the difference between a Latino and a Hispanic student? Rosa discovered that this process of forming ideas of race through ethnicity—something he labeled as *ethnoracial contortions*— was heavily informed by the ways in which institutions (such as the educational system as well as immigration) managed them. While both Puerto Ricans and Mexicans demonstrated an intimate knowledge and embrace of each other's culture, this relationship was persistently worn down by prevailing stereotypes and labels that came from authority figures and popular media. Over time, many of the students supported the claim that Puerto Ricans and Mexicans were racially different. And yet when Rosa asked some of the students how they would categorize romantic relationships between members of each group, most students would argue that these relationships were not to be considered interracial. Rosa relates this type of inconsistency to a larger theme of discussions on race:

> Many of the problems associated with the ethnographic documentation of racialization involve difficulty with the articulation of identity in the face of its theorization as a social construct. That is, if identity is socially constructed, then are we unable to locate and engage it analytically without merely reifying it?

One difference, for example, between race and ethnicity is that while ethnicity is described as a positive process in which groups are contributing members to a particular cultural or national group, race is seen as a more problematic process in which groups are seen as inherently unassimilable and distinct.

The process of labeling one group as a specific race is often driven by an effort to minimize their dignity in some manner. While there is an apparent lack of empirical validity in terms of using biology or ethnicity to organize people based on race, there is nonetheless a long and bloody history of dehumanizing different race groups as irrelevant or unworthy of consideration. Humanity has historically treated some people better than others based on purely visual criteria—especially that of the color of one's skin. This has led a large portion of our own species down a path of horrific persecution and internalized hatred. The inner conflict that has emerged from racism is illustrated brilliantly by W.E.B. Du Bois:

> The history of the American Negro is the history of this strife,—this longing to attain self-conscious manhood, to merge his double self into a better and truer self. In this merging he wishes neither of the older selves to be lost...He simply wishes to make it possible for a man to be both a Negro and an American…

The words of W.E.B. Du Bois speak to a certain and continued tragedy in modern times. Race has divided people for years, both between race groups and within race groups. Du Bois spoke of having two identities—of being forced to have a double consciousness. What does this mean? Black people were forced to constantly maintain an awareness over how they view themselves and how others view them. The oppressive systems of slavery and, later on, Jim Crow, forced those within it to view themselves through the eyes of White society—a society that looked at them with a great deal of contempt.

Recall our previous discussion on consciousness. Imagine, in Sartrean terms, throwing your consciousness outwards and finding only hatred and disgust towards your body and the color of your skin. How alienating would it be to not feel accepted—at home—on this Earth and in this body?

Although the White Europeans who focused on existentialism and phenomenology rarely mentioned race, their themes of anguish, dislocation, and existential uncertainty sadly also articulate the experience of being seen as the lesser Other. Toni Morrison, for example, wrote extensively on the feelings of ugliness and the rejection she felt as an African American woman. Her novel *The Bluest Eye* is the brilliant and heartbreaking story of a young Black girl named Pecola and her experience of being described as ugly due to her dark skin. This outer rejection is then internalized, leading to an obsession over having blue eyes—which is subtly equated with Pecola's striving towards attaining "Whiteness."

Postcolonial thinkers such as Frantz Fanon also took on the task of applying the existential crisis to the issue of race. In *Black Skin, White Masks*, Fanon offers a psychological interpretation of the same process of internalization experienced by Pecola. He observed that even from a young age, Black children were trained to associate Blackness with wrongness and Whiteness with goodness and purity.

Although we may like to act as if such issues are in the past—that racism has been solved—the default position of Whiteness as good or untouchable and the subordinate position of Blackness still persist. From beauty standards that place fair complexion, lightness, and Whiteness as the supreme features of an attractive person, to the self-evident police brutality against unarmed minorities in the United States, the issue of race is still quite in our backyard. The University of Pennsylvania, for example, found that racial minorities, especially Black individuals, were far more likely to experience police brutality when unarmed compared with White people. "Fatal police shootings are a public health emergency that contribute to poor health for BIPOC. Urgent attention from health professionals is needed to help drive policy efforts that reduce this unjust burden and move us towards achieving health equity in the US."

For people of color who must contend with the frustrating (if not utterly violent) persistence of subordination and discrimination, it would make sense to throw up one's hands and give up. Black nihilism represents such a stance. Whereas nihilism suggests the idea of having lost existentially affirming values, Black nihilism specifically centers on the despair and futility that Black people experience in trying to find a sustained and affirmed identity. At its extreme, this is seen in *afro-pessimism*, which seeks to "destroy the world," as it is a world that functions, essentially, on a logic of anti-Blackness.

Alternatively, we can look to thinkers like Fanon who provide a more hopeful alternative to such a dark (although fairly reasonable) outlook. Fanon saw each generation as responsible for achieving their historical mission or mode of existence. Of course, much of the success of this process is hinged upon the decisions of the past generations. And so the current generation is not operating in a vacuum. But to use Sartre's idea that "freedom is what you do with what has been done to you," Fanon likewise suggested that current Black generations should accept what has happened in the past and then encourage a process of collaboration, creativity, and revolution in order to create new values and forms of being.

To understand how to tackle racism, we must first understand its nature and characteristics. Here I will turn to Nietzsche's critique of two types of morality: the morality of the slave versus the morality of the master. The master, according to Nietzsche, sees goodness as that which is honorable and praiseworthy. In other words, they see goodness inherently within themselves. Badness, then, is found in mediocrity or weakness. While Nietzsche saw some use in this form of morality, he thought that it relied too heavily on old tropes and values and was, in a lot of ways, pretty facile. The master thinks he is good because he is good? Not a very strong argument to be made there.

And then there is slave morality. Nietzsche saw slave morality as a system in which goodness is found in weakness, resentment, and oppression. To be evil, under slave morality, is to be anything that is noble or strong. As Nietzsche writes:

> Here is the seat of the origin of the famous antithesis "good" and "evil":—power and dangerousness are assumed to reside in evil, a certain dreadfulness, subtlety, and strength, which do not admit of being despised. According to slave-morality, therefore, the "evil" man arouses fear; according to master-morality, it is precisely the "good" man who arouses fear and seeks to arouse it, while the bad man is regarded as the despicable being.

Racism is often a mix of the worst of both worlds. Bigots often simultaneously declare themselves to be better than the group that they are attacking (master morality) and also assert that they are being persecuted by the existence of such a "subhuman group." The master morality can be seen in racial supremacy movements today. The colonial project of Europe, for example, was hell-bent on subordinating and assimilating the weaker nature of indigenous peoples. The residential school system was developed as a means of "improving" the weaker and more primitive nature of those such as the Iroquois and Anishinaabe—signifying that they were too weak-minded and unintelligent to exist in modern society. The indigenous peoples were simultaneously seen as animalistic brutes that could attack "innocent" colonizers as well as uncivilized and undeveloped subhumans that must be educated.

Hitler, similarly, used rhetoric that made Jewish people sound like a group that was weighing down the potential of the German people. The Jewish people were simultaneously regarded as conspiring tricksters and less-than-human creatures. Another typical example is found with White supremacist groups (such as the KKK) that believe that they are inherently good based on the color of their skin. According to them, it is noble or right to be White. And to be Black is to be bad—weak or "less than" in some way. But Black people are often also characterized as a constant threat to peace and security—they must be subdued because they threaten the sanctity and purity of White society. The consequence of this, sadly, has been the continued lynching, public beating, and harassment of Black Americans based solely on the color of their skin. One of the clearest examples of the contradictory nature of racism is found in present-day characterizations of Mexican immigrants—who are simultaneously "lazy" and "dull" (and thus not masterful) and also take the job opportunities of well-meaning White citizens (and thus a threat to others). With the endless examples presented, it is apparent that the logic of racism and prejudice relies on contradictory evocations of victimhood and superiority to justify itself.

How does this contradiction, in which one views another group as equally strong and weak, come to be? Sartre viewed antisemites and racists not as practitioners of a coherent ideology but rather as individuals acting on a passion—something that is rooted in an irrational and emotional response. And so, the bigot feels compelled to justify knowingly spurious beliefs in an attempt to excuse their irrational proclivities. We see this nowadays with the edgy humor and dark jokes that flood message boards and chat rooms. These anonymous posters will use the justification that they are *just joking* in order to heinously attack other races and creeds. Sartre identified a connection between such bigotry and humor, found in the pleasure that the bigot derives from escaping the limits of reason. They enjoy and even experience fun in the practice of edgy humor. As Sartre notes, there might be a fundamental connection between humor and prejudice.

Of course, race is just one facet of identity that has been unjustly thrust upon people. While the embodied experience of racism has been greatly articulated through existentialism and phenomenology, it is not the only benefactor of those questioning what identity is. Intersectionality, the sociological approach to viewing people on the basis of several overlapping identity groups, has also demonstrated the importance of analyzing gender as a determinant of one's position in society and inner experience. What does it mean, for example, to be a Black woman or an Asian trans-man? Next, we turn to the fun and completely uncontroversial subject of gender.

Chapter 8

Gender

I have always found Heidegger's thrownness relevant to the subject of gender. Some of us are thrown into being men, some are thrown into being women, and some are thrown into something entirely different. And these roles tend to vary significantly in expression depending on time and place. Nonetheless, we are socially compelled to perform these roles. I was told as a child, for example, to play with dinosaur toys and to stay away from Barbies. At around the age of eight, I felt the need to prove that I was strong and good at sports when compared with my classmates. And around high school, I became conscious of the need to be perceived as a man—a good man. I needed to have a girlfriend, to be physically fit, and to have some amount of financial success.

Where does this compulsion come from? Thrownness is the experience of realizing that one has already become something specific. It is likely that you did not even realize you were playing the role of your gender until far later—as if the act itself was already predetermined. But thrownness goes beyond this. We are not only found to be a specific thing (a man or woman, for example). We also find ourselves, especially in modern times, thrown with no real reason or guarantee. Why are we to act in accordance with our gender roles?

This question was expertly taken up by Simone de Beauvoir (another existentialist) who asked "What is a woman?" As she understood, one is not born a woman but rather becomes a woman. This was perhaps one of the first popularizations of the sex-gender distinction, in which biological sex was seen as a natural and fundamental component to human development, and gender roles were seen as socially constructed forms of identity. For Beauvoir, this socially con-structed gender of femininity was one that always placed women in the role of the Other—of a group that is secondary to that of men. Men would treat women as a mystical Other who they simply could not understand. This is evident all the way back to ancient times, when the diagnosis of hysteria (derived from the Greek word *hystera* for "ovaries") was used to diagnose women whose behavior departed from commonly held social expectations.

Others have since taken on the task of clarifying what femininity is in the hopes of bettering the conditions of women everywhere. bell hooks expanded feminism to also touch upon the different experiences that women of color may have. This was done through intersectional feminism—an approach that applies the framework of intersectional-ity to examine how overlapping identities affect women's experiences of oppression. hooks noted, for example, that during times of slav-ery, White women were treated as "pure Goddess virgins," and Black women were treated as seductresses. These stereotypes contributed, simultaneously, to an infantilization of White women and the rape and devaluation of Black women. From this, hooks would lay her sights on the feminist movement itself and its lack of inclusivity, arguing that it failed to account for the specific needs of Black women that emerged through their particular historical treatment. Through her multilayered critiques, hooks made a considerable effort in creating a feminism for everybody in the hopes of freeing all from the oppressive shackles of sexism.

Judith Butler likewise expanded Beauvoir's inquiry into gender and greatly elaborated on the idea of "becoming" one's gender through the idea of gender performativity. For Butler, gender is a performance—something that is unstable and dependent on context. However, at the same time, gender finds its form in a stylized repetition of acts. I shave my beard every morning, I wear certain clothes, and I listen to aggressive music. Each day I do things that subtly confirm my own sense of gender identity.

Of course, I was born into a biologically male body, was assigned maleness at birth, and I identify as a man. But this isn't the case for others. The presence of trans individuals has opened up far more elaborate (and politically charged) discussions on what gender means. These individuals may experience a great deal of subjective inconsistency with how they feel about themselves and the bodies they inhabit. In short, it is an absolute incongruence between how one is perceived and who they feel they truly are. This can sometimes result in gender dysphoria, an experience linked to high suicide rates, substance abuse, and depression in which the sufferer is plagued by a deep sense of alienation and dislocation with their own sense of self.

While some may see the transgender experience as an inconsistency (how can gender be socially constructed if it also feels so innately essential?), I think it speaks to an important subtlety regarding any discussion on gender. Just because gender is performative or socially constructed does not mean that it is not ontologically important. Even Judith Butler specifies that their position surrounding gender as an "essential lie" nonetheless underscores the essentiality behind it:

> I do know that some people believe that I see gender as a "choice" rather than as an essential and firmly fixed sense of self. My view is actually not that. No matter whether one feels one's gendered and sexed reality to be firmly fixed or less so, every person should have the right to determine the legal and linguistic terms of their embodied lives. So whether one wants to be free to live out a "hard-wired" sense of sex or a more fluid sense of gender, is less important than the right to be free to live it out, without discrimination, harassment, injury, pathologization or criminalization—and with full institutional and community support.

Like race, gender does not lose its significance simply because of its lack of biological basis. Most of us do feel a strong inner pull towards certain forms of gender expression. To square this, the molecular biophysicist and trans activist Julia Serano proposed the *intrinsic inclination model*—a theory of gender that goes beyond either gender essentialism or pure social constructionism. Serano proposes that everyone has a relatively fixed sense of their own psychological sex, orientation, and also an inclination towards specific forms of gender expression. These interact with the larger social world and cultural standards to also help inform how someone expresses themselves. Serano goes on to suggest that, while most people tend to have a sexual expression, orientation, and gender that is relatively normative (straight masculine male, for example) there are plenty who vary across the spectrum.

No matter the case, I find Serano's idea of an intrinsic inclination—of something deeply essential to one's identity and yet not entirely biological-based—as a useful conceptualization of gender. Her theory is able to capture the diversity and fluidity found in gender expression while simultaneously avoiding any minimization of the importance of experiencing gender. She is able to incorporate both the inclusivity of social constructionism with the etiology of the biological sciences.

Chapter 9

Class

And finally, no matter what color, gender, or religion you are, your life is also undeniably dictated by the class you grew up in. There is a material reality to the world, one that runs on money and status. Born into the family of a billionaire? Sure, you may experience discrimination, prejudice, and hardship. But those things all hurt a little less when you know that you and your children's children will be well-fed. Similarly, born in a trailer park? You may make it out, but there's a far higher chance that your life will be plagued by financial instability and the threat of poverty.

And while everyone has their own struggles, regardless of how much money they have, those struggles will look quite different depending on class. Some would even argue that having an existential crisis is a sort of privileged struggle of higher classes—you can spend your time wallowing over ontological uncertainty while the rest of the world works two jobs. Most of the population has to reserve their energy to worry about their next paycheck. They can't afford any more dismay.

This may be why, for example, existentialism took root with the French bourgeoisie. Many of these thinkers could afford to spend long hours at the Café de Flore, waxing polemics over the human condition. The existential crisis signifies that one has time to catch their breath and look around. At least there's a small silver lining to all of this. The existentially anguished individual has been given the time and space to truly understand themselves and the world around them. And this is an incredibly important task that should not be diminished.

Thinkers who have been given ample opportunity to investigate and challenge the beliefs of their time often disseminate their ideas to the larger population. This, in turn, allows for the possibility of true social change. The existentialists changed the world through their uncompromised championing of authenticity and their critique of certain bourgeois assumptions. If they hadn't been afforded the space to question things, largely through financial stability, the world might be worse off for it.

While it isn't a prerequisite to have a trust fund—let alone financial stability—in order to experience an existential crisis (as will become apparent when we look at those in debt), I do think that this perspective highlights the silver lining behind having one. And it can definitely help with one of the more pernicious thoughts by which one might be tormented: "I shouldn't feel this bad when others have it so much worse."

At the end of the day, we are all struggling in our own ways. The category of class simply highlights why some may struggle with different aspects of existence when compared to others.[†]

But what is class exactly? For some thinkers, such as the French sociologist Pierre Bourdieu, it is everywhere. Class comes about through something he calls *habitus*, a cultural force that not only organizes our habits and routines throughout our lived experience but also structures how we perceive and judge these actions. It is "a historically structured, reproducing and durable ordering that refers to the maintenance of a class-divided social structure." Habitus is a shared experience—something that we all participate in and perpetuate through our shared social performance.

[†] Now, can we claim that some objectively have it worse than others? The issue of defining trauma and stress in terms of subjective perception versus objective criteria is a pernicious issue in the study of psychopathology, especially for those who suffer from post-traumatic stress disorder. More recent studies on adverse events and stress measures tend to look at the individual and dynamic interpretation of stress, but the jury is still out when discussing this controversial topic.

One area of habitus that is most obvious is in the notion of "taste." Taste can be seen as our ability to discern aesthetic value. To have good taste is to be able to distinguish between the simple and mainstream pleasures of popular culture and the genuine reflective enjoyment that stems from high culture. This is why, for example, some were horrified to discover that the 47th president was a fan of having his steak well done and eating McDonald's. Such a personal choice was, in fact, a political statement that signified his more populist taste despite identifying himself as an elite. This dietary preference demonstrated ignorance in what Bourdieu would describe as "cultural capital"—the codes that we use to exclude and distinguish ourselves and others based on social class. Even from what we choose to eat, drink, talk about, and watch—we already see the strength of class.

Of course, class does not only impact how we socialize and how pretentious we sound when discussing *foie gras*. It can also impact our health. To understand this, we first need to understand the role of stress in contributing to a wide range of health issues. When we are stressed—such as when we encounter a bear or discover that we have forgotten an important work assignment at home—we experience a wide range of physiological reactions. The cortex will activate our hypothalamus (the "fear" part of our brain), which then initiates our *fight-or-flight* response. Subsequently, our adrenal glands will secrete epinephrine. This lovely hormone, in turn, causes us to experience a whole host of unattractive symptoms. We sweat, our heart rate increases, and our pupils dilate.

This is all in preparation for our body to react against the stressor by energizing us to either fight or flee. This is healthy. The world is filled with dangers and uncertainties, and we do need to be prepared to handle them adequately. But what happens when we can't turn this system off? What if the stressors of the world never go away, or we feel like we can no longer handle them? This is the unfortunate experience of chronic stress—where we are in a constant state of fight-or-flight.

Chronic stress can be the root cause of many terrible health outcomes, including premature aging. With heightened cortisol release (another stress hormone), we see changes in the hippocampus, memory problems, high blood pressure, and a greater risk for obesity. Even worse, chronic stress tends to be associated with poor health habits that then contribute to worsening effects. We get stressed, eat junk food, and drink alcohol to calm ourselves, and this then worsens our physical well-being in the long run. What a terrible cycle!

The real kicker is that lower classes are overwhelmingly exposed to chronic stress. Study after study demonstrates that low socioeconomic status is significantly related to poor health outcomes, and the confounding variable is often stress. One classic study of British civil servants, for example, found that the lower the ranking of the workers, the worse off they were in terms of health outcomes. The researchers labeled this phenomenon as "status syndrome"—finding that the status of each servant was largely intertwined with mortality rates. And after measuring cortisol rates in the morning, they concluded that the main contributor was that the lower the rank, the higher the stress.

When we consider the importance of financial security, this finding begins to make sense. Lower-class folk tend to have less stability, certainty, and agency in their lives. An unexpected bill or having to compromise one's time with loved ones for a paycheck are just a few examples that could demonstrate all of the nefarious ways in which a lack of money results in increased misery. As a consequence of financial insecurity, a great deal of autonomy and sense of agency is compromised. A slight increase in food prices, an unexpected illness that keeps a wage earner home from work, or the potential loss of a job can keep one in a chronic state of anxiety and danger. Those of lower socioeconomic status, more often than not, find themselves in a state of chronic uncertainty due to the lack of financial stability that marks their lives. While money may not buy us happiness, it certainly helps us from feeling constantly miserable!

Like gender and race, money can be a surprisingly strong influence on how we feel about our lives. And this is in spite of its nature as a largely socially constructed concept. Thinkers such as Yuval Noah Harari have gone to great lengths in explaining the simple and yet often forgotten fact that money is a shared fiction. In other words, it is something that we have collectively agreed to give value and meaning to. The relative value of money as a concept is only as real as we collectively decide it is. Which, in theory, sounds quite nice. But this does not mean that we can simply pretend that money does not matter. Money often feels *very* real and can actually be the source of a great deal of anguish and anxiety. This is evident in the brutally powerful influence of debt on our identities. The millions of young college students who are hundreds of thousands of dollars in debt can attest to the ability of money to bring forth an existential crisis. The sort of debt that is accrued can feel like it is inextricably linked to who one is. David J. Blacker, a professor of philosophy at the University of Delaware, writes about this type of ontological nightmare with astounding clarity:

> After having acquired it, one is "stuck" with one's educational purchase as decisively as one is stuck with one's own vital organs. What this means is that an inseparable and non-isolable part of oneself is the debt generating culprit; in this case, one does not owe a debt for the car or for the goods purchased via credit card, but rather one owes educational debt against oneself or, more precisely, against what one has become. One might call this species of debt existential, a kind of debt from which it is impossible to separate one's very continued existence.

Debt effectively ties the past to the present and the future. Your wishes and desires will now be weighed heavily against your ability to pay off those loans and debts. Debt has an impressive ability to shrink one's future into an existence of purely economic decision-making. For example, a change of the heart that urges you away from becoming a medical surgeon and instead towards a writing career can now be effectively silenced. You'll still need to pay off medical school.

This is reminiscent of the anarchist anthropologist David Graeber's critique of economic theory as a whole—it limits what it means to be a human being. Instead of complex and ever-changing entities, the individual now becomes a "Homo economicus"—an economic unit driven by rational cost-benefit analysis. Graeber sees money and debt as effectively corroding what we value. Value, in the sociological sense, is a matter of valuing what one feels is *ultimately good* or *desirable* for human life. The sociological view of value sees the good life as the central aim of our existence. It is all of those special things that we simply cannot put a price on.

Alternatively, as Graeber argues, value is often considered in terms of its return on investment. Goals, decisions, and exchanges are weighed in reference to how much one receives in comparison to how much one has given away or sacrificed. As we grow older, we may feel inclined to value things more and more in an economic sense. And with the mounting pile of debt that plagues a considerable amount of twentysomethings across North America, we will likely see more and more stressed-out and anxious individuals forced into viewing their lives as something that is little more than a vessel towards paying off a loan.

Chapter 10

What's Been Done to You

For some, money may come to entirely define and dominate their life. We could spend our few years on Earth paying off that loan instead of truly creating a life of our own. For others, it may be an uncompromising commitment to strict gender roles. We could spend our precious time trying to impress others in the hopes of convincing them that we are something that we are not. Whatever the case, it is clear that what has been done to us, if we fail to become aware of it, runs the risk of controlling our lives. The important next step, then, is to become aware of these factors. Psychologist Carl Jung asserted, "The psychological rule says that when an inner situation is not made conscious, it happens outside, as fate." In other words, until we gain some clarity and acceptance in terms of who we have been defined as, we will continue to be shaped and molded by these features of our identity. We will continue to be controlled by our past.

An existential crisis can be seen as an opportunity to free oneself from the shackles of our inner situation—of those expectations and assumptions we have made about ourselves that dominate our lives. As has been demonstrated in our inquiries into gender, race, class, and all of the other constitutive elements of the self, an existential crisis can emerge from those ways in which seemingly stable aspects of the self—these elements of contingency that we have been thrown into— are suddenly problematized. It can feel as if we have been left entirely at odds with ourselves and the world around us. Such an experience can be quite unsettling, and you may certainly feel like this whole project of discovering who you are is all for naught. Depression may, in fact, come knocking at your door. And, of course, nobody should seek out experiences that will actively leave them distressed and depressed.

But I would also propose that this alienating encounter with the self is merely the first step on an exciting journey—one that can bring you closer to recognizing the malleability inherent in those seemingly static features that make up who we are.

Of course, what has been done to us (socially, genetically, biologically, politically, and so on) cannot be altered. They occurred in the past. But this does not mean that we are required to continue along these premade paths. Nor does it mean that we must radically alter everything about who we are. We may, in fact, have some say in who we might be. Of course, this investigation into contingency should offer us a space of temporary respite, to catch our breath and accept that, yes, some things cannot be changed. Your childhood. How others have treated you. How much money you currently have.

But also, just as importantly, understanding this contingency should open up our eyes to the fact that some things aren't quite as they appear to be. Some aspects of identity that we have clung on to are now put into question. What we have been told about who we are should be questioned. And how we view others should be challenged and interrogated. While you may be more confused about who you are than ever before, recognize this as the first step in an exciting journey towards becoming all of those things that you never knew you could be.

Part 2

Making Oneself

In this part, we investigate how identity is formed. This involves looking at the process of forming identity itself and how technology has changed how we see ourselves. We will also look at how we may compromise ourselves along the process of making ourselves—especially from a young age when we must choose between being authentic and feeling connected to others.

Class, race, gender, personality, whether you're double-jointed or not—certainly you've inherited quite an identity. The previous section was an attempt to categorize and explore a short list of these inherited components. But are they inherited? Of course, it could be useful to split these constituent elements of identity into those that are "achieved" versus those that are "ascribed." We tend to choose our careers and partners (we achieved them). And we tend to find ourselves ascribed to certain religions and with certain genetic variations (we have been ascribed to them). But what about arranged marriages? What about mutations in protein folding that change our gene expression? These aspects of our identity aren't entirely solid, and even constraining them to the categories of nature versus nurture or social versus biological doesn't seem to help. And so for the purposes of discussion, we have lumped them together.

And how do these aspects of our identity determine our life course? Depending on your class level, you could be destined for a life of chronic health issues. Depending on your race, you could be burdened with double consciousness and live in constant comparison with others. Moreover, depending on your sex or gender, you'll likely inherit a whole host of issues, such as harassment, period cramps, and the prospect of childbirth—experiences that you would have never encountered as a man. Clearly, our identities do not give us a fair chance. Some will have it better than others. And, of course, what "better" means largely depends on time and place.

The next question that should be raised for anyone going through an existential crisis is the extent to which one should identify with these seemingly *stable* features of identity. Because, as we've seen, these features are far less stable than we may have assumed. They change with context. As the world changes around us, we change in tandem. Our sense of self is intimately tied with society at large. To manage this, we often need to reserve aspects of ourselves to private moments or perhaps only around a few trusted loved ones. This reflects the consequences of that formidable "Me" phase of child development, where we become socially conscious of our placement in a world of others. How do we accomplish this task of balancing who we are and how we are seen? This is a question taken up by the sociologist Niklas Luhman, who asked, "How far can the internal self and external persona be united?" This, according to Luhman, is the "problem of identity"—while we need some sort of ontological certainty and coherent sense of self, it isn't obvious the extent to which this self must cohere with a more socially acceptable self. How do we make an identity?

As we have already seen, many aspects of identity—such as gender and race—are already quite context-dependent. But what if the very construct of identity-making has changed and transformed through time? Well, that is very much the case. Next, we will go over the different ways in which identity has been formed throughout history. As we will see, how we have approached identity through time has shifted considerably, and now more than ever, identity has become a fraught and confusing construct. Of course, it wasn't always that way…

Chapter 11

Sincerity

Let's keep it simple.

What if who we were on the outside was who we actually were? What if there was perfect congruence between our actual feeling and what we confess to be? This is Lionel Trilling's concept of "sincerity," which he argued to be the core morality of pre-Enlightenment (premodern) society. To be sincere is to commit to one's social roles earnestly. In this sense, one could point to no real inner core. Strip the layers of your identity back further and further, and what you have left is an apparent emptiness. This is to say that, under sincerity, we are solely our social roles and that by which society views us as. As the philosophers Hans-Georg Moeller and Paul D'Ambrosio explain:

> Under conditions of sincerity, a dual correspondence is often required. One should not only act in accordance with one's roles but also endorse one's actions psychologically. In this way, one honestly identifies with one's roles. In this view, moreover, it is generally assumed that if everyone does so, harmonious interactions and social stability will follow.

In simple terms, people in premodern times endorsed who they were because doing so kept things running smoothly. A wife was a wife. A servant was a servant. And this maintained the social fabric for quite some time. I mean, imagine what would happen if the peasant began identifying as a real human being with rights and the desire for political expression. That would end in a bloody revolution! And so many, throughout time, stuck fervently to their social role, either out of a genuine interest in preserving social order or due to external threats.

One of the positives of sincerity lies in its ability to quell anxiety and despair over who we are and how free we feel. Having an existential crisis was less likely to happen in that day and age, presumably because there was less flexibility (and thus freedom) regarding who you could become. Your identity was firmly tied to society, and, on some level, it must have been quite nice. You might have worked long hours on your family farm, but at least you had already accepted the fact that this was your life. You could sleep at night knowing this is who you are and will always be. Under sincerity, those aspects of our identity that we had little say in became far more tolerable when they were seen less as restriction and more as fate or destiny.

In these earlier premodern times, sincerity relied on the initial premise that who one was internally was the same as who they were in the social world. Eventually, however, certain misalignments would develop between society and the individual. Some individuals, especially those given especially harsh treatment based on their identity (such as women and minorities), took issue with how the system was being run. Sure, the social fabric was in order. But for whom? And how could one possibly have their inner psychology perfectly aligned with society? Moeller and D'Ambrosio further explain this inner tension experienced in the Age of Sincerity, "At the heart of all these issues… is the impossible demand for a person's inner psychology to become fully congruent with external social expectations."

Family fights, divorces, suicides, and even violent rebellions all signified an incompatibility with aspects of individual identity and social identity. Clearly, the system of sincerity did not entirely account for what would make for a satisfying identity or form of self-hood. Our inner desires and inclinations are in perpetual tension with the norms and demands of the social world.

This is where, for example, the school of psychoanalysis developed to examine what was repressed and subordinated by cultural norms. In a society as rigid and prudish as late-eighteenth-century Europe, it was fairly predictable that those such as Freud would find the private desires for sexual liberation at odds with the larger social world. Repression, the unconscious blocking of unwanted and shameful thoughts, was the last tool that the "sincere" individual could use in the face of conformity and social pressure. Something was ready to burst—the authentic self in all its messy and peculiar glory.

Chapter 12

Authenticity

This is Lionel Trilling's second stage of identity-building that emerged from the apparent shortcomings of sincerity. Associated primarily with the Romantic period of the late 1700s, the Age of Authenticity championed prioritizing one's unique self or inner core above all else. Rather than being composed of a bunch of social roles you have inherited, authenticity is aligned with the view of some sort of essential self that could be unlocked or uncovered if we really learn to *follow our heart*. Where sincerity valued externally imposed identity roles, authenticity placed "being yourself" as the main prerogative. According to Trilling, being authentic involves staying true to oneself, even if it means going against what is considered socially acceptable. "Be original" and "Become who you are" emerged as the slogans of the time.

Even now, many would argue that authenticity and the imperative to be true to yourself is still the reigning form of identity-building. Such language is plastered on Nike ads and is prevalent across all forms of TV shows, popular books, and self-help podcasts. And, importantly, it reflects the idea that we are always trying to be what we are not.

After all, the best way to demonstrate authenticity is to act in polar opposition to trends and the conforming masses. Then you will be yourself, right? But unlike the Age of Sincerity, authenticity requires a great deal more effort on the part of the individual in search of an identity. Take, for example, a hot dog. A hot dog is made with some sort of meaning or purpose in mind—to be eaten and enjoyed. Similarly, the Age of Sincerity treated humans like hot dogs. There's (mostly) only one clear use for a hot dog. For the hot dog and the premodern human, essence precedes existence. Humans were born with some predetermined pathway. They were to follow prewritten scripts and adequately hit every mark along the way. And this was all the more possible with the notion of a god, who created us in accordance with his Divine Plan. Even in times of doubt, we could feel confident knowing we had a purpose.

This explains why Nietzsche's declaration that "God is dead and we have killed him" is less of a celebration and more of an ominous warning. Without God, we are forced to reckon with the possibility that we were put on this Earth for little rhyme or reason—that the roles we are thrown into are fairly arbitrary. We find, unlike the hot dog, that existence precedes our essence. We are hot dogs without buns, floating aimlessly in space! We must find our purpose! Or in the words of Nietzsche, we must become who we are and forge an identity in the face of this meaningless existence.

This is a lifelong journey for many and could include periods of intense anxiety, confusion, and despair that some might call an identity crisis. Left to your own devices, who are you truly? This anxiety—"the dizziness of freedom," as Kierkegaard famously put it—became the hallmark of existential thought. To paraphrase Sartre and Beauvoir, *we are condemned to be free*. Our freedom to choose our own path, create ourselves, and operate essentially with no objective purpose became the fundamental question posed to the individual.

Of course, the celebration of subjectivity and individual authenticity was hardly met with unanimous appraisal. Even now, more traditionally minded figures, such as Jordan Peterson—who advocate for more rigid social roles in terms of gender and vocation—argue that an overemphasis on individuality threatens social stability. He writes on his site:

> Your identity is not the clothes you wear, or the fashionable sexual preference or behaviour you adopt and flaunt, or the causes driving

your activism, or your moral outrage at ideas that differ from yours: properly understood, it's a set of complex compromises between the individual and society as to how the former and the latter might mutually support one another in a sustainable, long-term manner. It's nothing to alter lightly, as such compromise is very difficult to attain, constituting as it does the essence of civilization itself, which took eons to establish, and understanding, as we should, that the alternative to the adoption of socially-acceptable roles is conflict— plain, simple and continual, as well as simultaneously psychological and social.

Those like Peterson see the identity crisis among younger people as evidence of this widescale abandonment of traditional sincerity. This process, they believe, has threatened the social fabric through "confusing everyone." While reverting to a period of rigid social roles may be an impossibility and something that most would likely rather not do, I think these conservative thinkers still raise an interesting point regarding authenticity. With authenticity comes the risk of nihilism and despair. It can become increasingly hard to understand who we should become with no frame of reference. This is that heavy responsibility that the existentialists warned about—that freedom is both a blessing and a curse. How do we know that what we are doing is correct or matters in the end?

The process of creating one's identity can feel futile at times. While we try our best to follow our own heart, we more often than not find ourselves choosing the paths of others. With so many choices, where do we turn? What do we pick? Ernest Becker illustrates it here:

> When we are young, we are often puzzled by the fact that each person we admire seems to have a different version of what life ought to be, what a good man is, how to live, and so on. If we are especially sensitive it seems more than puzzling, it is disheartening. What most

people usually do is follow one person's ideas and then others depending on who looms largest on one's horizon at the time. The one with the deepest voice, the strongest appearance, the most authority and success, is usually the one who gets our momentary allegiance; and we try to pattern our ideals after him. But as life goes on, we get a perspective on this, and all these different versions of truth become a little pathetic. Each person thinks that he has the formula for triumphing over life's limitations and knows with authority what it means to be a man, and he usually tries to win a following for his particular patent.

This is an inherent contradiction in authenticity. We are told to be ourselves, but how we define who we are is still fundamentally rooted in reference to others. Some may describe this as a relationship with the Other. How is our sense of self reliant on the Other? Firstly, somehow defining oneself in a vacuum, with no reference to anyone else, can be quite a challenge! This almost takes on the same difficulty as the task of developing a new type of color without any reference to any previously existing color. Identity, likewise, often relies on some referent to form itself around.

This relationship with identity-making and the Other is evident in anthropologist Gregory Bateson's work on how different communities form their identities through the presence of other communities. Many times, neighboring societies appear to develop in deliberate contrast with each other—perhaps a reflection of the need to use the Other as a symbol of what is nonhuman. Anthropologists such as Bateson describe this process as *schismogenesis*—the formation of cultures through difference. They define themselves through the Other. This is apparent in large cultural differences—such as those between France, Spain, and Italy—and countries where the difference (at first glance) appears smaller. Many Canadians, for example, are known to define themselves, first and foremost, as being not Americans. Different cultures develop in opposition to one another. The Other represents what we are not or would not like to be. And so we develop an identity in contrast to the Other.

We also rely on others for our own subsistence. In other words, we need others to survive on a biological and material level. We rely on shipping, health services, and our caregivers to take care of us and ensure we are nourished. The interdependence of the self with the world around it is perhaps best summed up by the philosopher Bruno Latour's distinction between *autotrophs* and *heterotrophs*. Latour views the Earth as an overlapping and connecting assemblage of heterotrophs. A heterotroph is something that depends on a phantom body—a network of interacting elements that it needs to satisfy its existence. Heterotrophs, in simple terms, depend on others for survival. This is compared to autotrophs—beings that can subsist entirely independently. Despite our human desire to "be an individual" and identify with the autotroph, Latour argues that we are actually the furthest from such a claim of individual sovereignty. This was exemplified by the COVID-19 pandemic, in which many of us were suddenly struck with the disturbing insight that our daily existence largely depends on an entire global network of others. Latour writes:

> We couldn't long survive without a whole host of jobs of which we had till then, we must admit, only a fairly vague awareness of: catering jobs, deliverers, carriers, not to mention nurses, ambulance drivers and carers, a whole tribe of people as poorly paid as they were poorly viewed. Carrying out the simplest course of action like feeding yourself requires the support of quite a few agents to "ensure continuity" of the most ordinary life.

Aside from the few extreme libertarians who can live in the woods (and even then, they live *off* of the woods and its ecosystem), we are *heterotrophic*—our survival fundamentally relies on others. Where we end and others begin (others including not only other humans but animals, plants, and the elements) isn't entirely clear. Individualism is a nice idea, but relatively illusory on a biological level. And so Latour, in a call to action that could evoke claustrophobia, asks us to "stop thinking in terms of identity and start thinking in terms of overlapping and encroachment."

A Few Words on Compromising Ourselves

An awareness of the importance of the Other in developing a sense of self is essential in furthering self-knowledge. However, there also is a risk in taking this reliance entirely on the Other too far. Where is the line between attaching ourselves to others for a sense of security and claiming some independence in order to assert our own selfhood?

As demonstrated, it is quite difficult to express ourselves entirely because we rely on and are responsible to others. We must often compromise our originality or uniqueness bit by bit if we are to function socially. The tension between being authentic and attaching to others begins in childhood and remains throughout life. This is a central observation in the work of addiction specialist Gabor Maté. From the first instance we are told not to do something we feel naturally inclined to do (cry, play, or laugh), we make a choice to risk losing care and affection from our caregivers by being "true" to ourselves. More often than not, we choose attachment, as this guarantees our survival. Over time, however, we may learn to consistently favor and consider the needs of others over our own, leading to a sort of people-pleasing personality that is linked to chronic illness and adverse relationship outcomes.

We learn from a young age that to be oneself—to be messy, ugly, needy, and stupid—isn't loveable. Crying because we feel hurt or launching into a temper tantrum is met with the disapproval of our caretakers. Children learn to be accepted not for who they are but for how they are. Their worth is dictated by their behavior. Later on, we

note that being too vulnerable or weird drives away romantic prospects. What we are left with is an ultimatum: You can either be yourself
or you can be loved.

And so, our relationships become cyclical. We compromise in the
beginning, prioritizing attachment over authenticity. We tuck away
ourselves, repressing the emotions that feel closest to us. But this only
lasts a short while. Sooner or later, ugly truths violently crash through
our frozen surface of conformity. We risk a divorce, a breakup, and the
severing of ties with our family members. However, after some time
passes and our solitude grows intolerable, we find ourselves once again
repressing who we are to be with others.

Is this cycle an inevitability? Can we resolve the tension between
authenticity and attachment? "Most of our tensions and frustrations
stem from compulsive needs to act the role of someone we are not,"
writes János Selye. This has become increasingly more evident when
we look at medical research. When we think of an unhealthy personality, we tend to imagine a stressed-out CEO who is unwilling to make
time for his family or to simply slow down. Although this personality
type has its own risks, recent studies suggest a far more insidious trait
that many of us carry. As Maté notes, those who tend to compulsively
place others' expectations and needs ahead of their own are more likely
to end up with chronic illnesses. "It struck me that these patients had a
higher likelihood of cancer and poorer prognosis...repression disarms
one's ability to protect oneself from stress."

These highly toxic repressive personality traits include a compulsive
concern for others, a rigid identification with responsibility and duty,
a repression of healthy self-protective aggression, and the consistent
acting out of two beliefs: *I am responsible for how other people feel*,
and *I must never disappoint anyone*. Of course, none of these traits are
inherently bad, but Maté notes that the compulsive nature of such behaviors denotes a health risk. He explains further: "These dangerously
self-denying traits tend to fly under our radar because they are easily

conflated with their healthy analogues: compassion, honor, diligence, loving, kindness, generosity…"

One issue with being so overly considerate and agreeable is that having such traits is socially desirable. They are likable. For those who wish to be liked, acting in an overly agreeable and giving manner is an easy gateway into general acceptability. In other words, we tend to adopt these behaviors not out of a sincere sense of compassion but rather as a way to be liked, to feel attached and accepted. We may even place our health at risk in order to be worthy of love. This explains the overrepresentation of women with chronic illnesses, who are usually socialized at a young age to repress their emotions and satisfy the needs of others over their own. More generally, Maté explains how such a personality could develop:

> If our environment cannot support our gut feelings and our emotions, then the child, in order to 'belong' and 'fit in' will automatically, unwittingly and unconsciously, suppress their emotions and their connections to themselves, for the sake of staying connected to the nurturing environment, without which the child cannot survive. A lot of children are in this dilemma – 'can I feel and express what I feel or do I have to suppress that in order to be acceptable, to be a good kid, to be a nice kid?'

The child, pretty much entirely unable to survive without social support, learns to prioritize attachment over authenticity. Learning what our parents want from us becomes an adaptive survival response—one that we maintain as we grow up. We learn that to be inauthentic is to survive. Here, Maté criticizes Jordan Peterson, who recommends punishing any outbursts from the child through isolation and scorn, teaching the child that any negative emotion should be repressed lest they risk severance from their loved ones. From this, we may develop an overly agreeable exoskeleton that surpasses any need for setting boundaries. We may also begin to internalize the aspirations of those around us, prioritizing external validation over internal validation. Maté elaborates further that it is "better to believe 'It's my fault; I'm bad,' which lets you believe there's the chance that 'if I work hard and be good, I will be loveable.' Thus, even the debilitating belief in one's unworthiness…begins as a coping mechanism…" It becomes inconceivable that those entrusted to care for us are fundamentally bad, as our survival depends on them. Instead, we must view ourselves as inherently bad, and thus it is our job to become acceptable and, consequently, loved.

Chapter 13

E-Authenticity

Maté and others posit the importance of authenticity in reclaiming one's identity. To compromise who one is—whatever this may mean—is evidently unhealthy. Some, however, may argue that Maté's position is outdated. How can we truly remain authentically ourselves when the social world is constantly evolving and shifting? After all, we do need to base our identity on some aspects of the social world—whether it's the clothes we wear or our political beliefs. I look at my own work as a writer and YouTuber as an example of this. I have tried to remain authentic, but what that means has shifted considerably throughout my career. I have made several attempts (with varying degrees of success) to relate to my audience and show my own vulnerable side.

While I began my channel with a focus on purely educational content, such as short guides to philosophical schools and thinkers, I soon grew exhausted over the fairly unfulfilling process of making such content. And the audience did, too! Views were down. The demand for such videos changed. Here, I found it hard to tell exactly where I compromised my authentic desire to teach philosophy and where I authentically felt the need to make different content. I felt, implicitly, that I needed to express myself and make something that would connect with others. But I also felt the external pressure to make new content.

Around the same time, I went through my first real breakup. As I tend to do, I took my thoughts to the Notes app and wrote out a heartfelt message that I would never send to my ex. It was a letter of sorts, commemorating our relationship, reflecting on the insecurity of singleness, confessing my desire to love them, and expressing the difficulties of accepting that things simply weren't meant to be. With little reflection on what would happen next, I decided to turn the letter into the script for a video titled "for her." When I uploaded the video, I assumed the content would be met with mixed or even negative feedback. Where is the philosophy content? But that's not how things turned out. The video is currently one of my most popular and sits at around three million views as I write this. Why?

People like vulnerability and are drawn to a sort of authenticity. This sort of authenticity nostalgia is highly marketable because it hits people right in their feelings. Thousands of comments poured out over "for her"—mostly reflecting a sense of shared heartbreak and struggle in their own breakups. I gave a bit of myself to others. And it was a nice feeling, far more fulfilling than making educational content. But then I felt a strange pressure—I must be authentic no matter what. This is, after all, my livelihood.

This is the principle behind Eva Illouz's *emotional capitalism*, where affect has become a central feature of our economy. Shed a tear! Laugh with joy! To be emotional is to signify some sort of authenticity and disclose one's personal journey towards fulfillment. This is a highly profitable venture. And in a less cynical sense, it offers a sense of connection with others. If I am authentic to a wide audience, I can foster a sense of belonging or relationship with this audience. However, at the end of the day, this audience is still a group of paying customers. And so the imperative to "be myself" becomes central to my material existence. This is perhaps best captured by Byung-Chul Han's argument that neoliberalism forces us to see ourselves, our identities, no longer as subjects but instead as projects to be worked on and marketed: "But now the illusion prevails that every person—as a project free to fashion him or herself at will—is capable of unlimited self-production."

Yes, the success of this more *authentic* chapter on YouTube gave me a sense of validation regarding who I was. The channel grew beyond anything I could have ever imagined. But over the years, I began to experience the sort of burnout that Han describes. That many eyeballs on me emphasized the importance of pushing out authentic content and being *true to myself*. Each video was a part of myself that, upon publication, was to be ranked and monetized, consumed, and thrown back out into the digital void. There was only so much I could handle in terms of constantly commodifying myself. I experienced a strange existential crisis—in which I no longer identified, and even dreaded, those aspects of myself that I used to champion as being entirely *me*. This is why, perhaps, so many influencers and content creators complain about burnout as a symptom of the content mill. Han continues: "The ego grows exhausted and wears itself down; such tiredness stems from the redundancy and recurrence of the ego." This overemphasis on the self and the subsequent process of commodifying it through content places one in a tenuous relationship with one's identity. What does it mean to be authentic when so much of our personality is staked on analytics and the wishes of our audience?

Chapter 14

Profilicity

This is Moeller and D'Ambrosio's main contribution to the history of identity-building: *profilicity*.

In simple terms, profilicity is prioritizing one's profile as central to identity. Compared with sincerity, which centers around our social roles, and authenticity, which centers around our essential self, profilicity seeks only general acclaim and the ability to capture attention. Without this attention—this rendering of one's existence through a profile—it is difficult to claim that such an existence is worthwhile. A mother sharing an intimate and incredibly *authentic* moment with her child may nonetheless feel compelled to share this moment with her Instagram followers. If nobody can like or react to such a moment, did it ever really happen? Moeller applies the Nietzschean motto of "Become who you are," which reflects the core tenets of authenticity, to his concept of profilicity: "Become who you wish to be seen as."

How did this come to be? With modernity, we have become less and less motivated to observe things under primary analysis. Social media and technology have now made it quite easy to sort through tons of information in order to come to a decision. This is largely thanks to *second-order observation*. Decades ago, we might have asked out someone at a coffee shop because we thought they were cute. Perhaps we would have applied to a school because it is close and the campus is nice. Now, through the advancement of modern technology, and the pressure to do things as quickly as possible, we favor second-order observation as a means of making such decisions. In modern times, we tend to observe things as they have already been "observed" or measured by some external source. Instead of seeking a cute date at a coffee shop, we might use dating apps to sort romantic prospects for us algorithmically. We might use the number of followers that a romantic prospect has on Instagram in order to confirm their relative worth as a partner. Instead of having to know about a university program personally, we can now peruse internet forums and online rankings to determine which school is the best under specific criteria.

This whole system relies on profiles: units of information that are curated to tell us how others value a certain object of interest (a restaurant, an Airbnb, ourselves). Profiles do not have any essential value to them. Instead, they derive their value in relation to other profiles. Being original no longer matters. What matters now, for example, is that you are "more original" than someone else (whatever this may mean). Profilicity, then, is a matter of attention and acclaim, of sticking out regardless of whether you internally feel like you are being who you are. It's also quite distinct from notions of sincerity, as societal expectations are ever-changing and, as a result, how profiles are ranked changes at an equally constant rate.

Presently, we are less likely to form our identities based on being true to ourselves. Instead, we develop an identity under the system of profiles (or profilicity). Interestingly, Moeller and D'Ambrosio do not consider this a sort of tragedy or dystopian nightmare. Rather, they see this new form of identity-making as a natural progression from authenticity—a reaction to a world that is becoming increasingly reliant on speed and efficiency. We are not truly one thing or another unless it has been Tweeted, posted, or rated by what Moeller and D'Ambrosio call the "general peer"—the faceless, anonymous mass of online audiences. This is the new Other. So, being authentic or sincere becomes less important than being seen—in being ranked and sorted concerning other identity profiles.

Chapter 15

The Identity Crisis

All three types of identity formation—sincerity, authenticity, and pro-filicity—come with their pitfalls. While *sincerity* brings with it a severe lack of inclusion, and *authenticity* brings with it anxiety and confusion, an overidentification with one's profile can also result in a constant need to conform one's personal life with one's outward appearance. The general peer can weigh quite heavily into who one decides to be. I found myself in this position as I came to overidentify with my online personality. I felt the compulsion to be a wise, moralistic sage in my everyday life. If a friend had some sort of personal issue, I experienced a deep urge to wax philosophical and psychologize in order to help them see the light. And as my content grew more political, I felt that I, too, needed to reflect my social stances in terms of lifestyle and who I associated with. I became closer friends with Leftists and began to actively reject large offers of money if I felt my "values" were being compromised.

But were these my values? Whose values are these exactly? Mine or my audience or some sort of larger political ideal? For the first time since high school, I experienced a severe identity crisis. I felt like I couldn't properly grasp any stable aspect of identity—let alone comfortably pursue an authentic or sincere life. Who was I? I took a step back from YouTube. I traveled. I meditated. And I entered ther-apy. Broadly, I clued in on one damaging aspect of how I saw myself. *I take myself too seriously.* Strange, right? Shouldn't you take yourself seriously? After all, you are all who you will be for the rest of your life. This was where I began to understand the damage of *overidentification*.

As I discovered, those aspects of the self that I have been thrown into (my humanness, my gender, my class) were far too unstable to claim entirely as core components of my being. Even what I decided to take seriously—my essential self, my online profile—all led to paradox and uncertainty. Whether it was an inability to "form my own values" under authenticity or the audience's experience in profilicity, such forms of identity-making also failed to offer that ontological certainty. I felt this imperative to form a strong and stable identity. But what if this was the wrong approach? What if, instead, I should spend time weakening these powerful self-beliefs that form a sense of who I am?

And so I spent hours (and thousands of dollars) under schema therapy—a form of therapy that seeks to disentangle and examine those beliefs we tell ourselves *about ourselves* from an early age. These beliefs and stories may have been useful at a certain time in childhood. But now they have worn out their welcome. They may impede happiness and lead to paths of misery and alienation. And I discovered that many of the stories I told myself were horror stories. For example, I discovered that I had a schema of perfectionism. This manifested in the story I would retell in every test center and basketball game: *I need to perform perfectly, or I will not be loved.* Along these lines, I also had the schema of emotional inhibition—a fear of truly opening up. How ironic! That had been my entire career.

But was I really opening up, or had I been simply trained to disclose those parts of myself that would give me praise and views? Emotional inhibition relies on the same schematic narrative as perfectionism: *I need to show no vulnerability, or I will not be loved.* And this all stemmed from a larger schema (a meta-schema in some sense). *Defectiveness*— an inchoate anxiety that, deep down, beyond all social roles and aspects of my identity, beyond all the achievements and accolades, I was fundamentally unlovable. There was an inner emptiness—a sense of nothingness that I was covering up with an acceptable persona. Defectiveness revealed a profound drive that had taken control over much of my life. I was motivated to build this persona—this identity—in order to hide the ugliness within.

Of course, by revealing these schemas, we weaken their strength. There is a hidden and implicit element to schemas that can nefariously control much of our everyday life without us ever quite knowing. Much of schema therapy is spent bringing these schemas into the light and then logically debunking the supposed truthfulness behind such claims. Will people stop loving me if I fail an exam? Probably not. Can opening up sometimes help rather than hurt my relationships? Probably.

Most importantly, what were my standards for determining whether I was defective? Was I really all that unlovable? With time, I loosened up the knots of my identity—of these seemingly stable narratives and self-beliefs that were holding me back. And it was a refreshing experience in some sense. I felt again that taste of true ontological freedom that first drew me into reading about existentialism.

Ah, yes, I was condemned to be free. But was there a proper way to carry out this condemnation? How am I to use this freedom exactly? While therapy allowed me to loosen up my sense of self, I still had to contend with the need for some sort of existential security. Beyond these self-beliefs, my profile, misplaced sense of authenticity, and sincere social roles—who was I really?

Chapter 16

Genuine Pretending

This task of defining oneself, without overly identifying with one aspect of identity or another, is a tricky one. In each stage of identity formation that we looked at, there is an apparent level of overidentification with one's identity. Be too sincere, and we risk losing everything about ourselves. Be too authentic, and we find ourselves anxiety-ridden and paranoid over any possible infringement. And when we become too prolific, we become a vessel of the algorithm with little of ourselves left. Moeller and D'Ambrosio offer a useful counterbalance to such an issue, found in Taoist philosophy: *genuine pretending*.

Zhuangzi was an influential Chinese philosopher—best known for writing a text that is also called the *Zhuangzi*. This ancient text sets out to use humor and fantastical storytelling to challenge the arbitrariness of dichotomies we have come to accept as normal (good and evil, life and death, Self and Other). In one of its more famous stories, the protagonist, Zhuang Zhou, dreams of being a butterfly. While he is a butterfly, he does not know he is Zhuang Zhou.

Suddenly, he woke up, and there he was, solid and unmistakable Zhuang Zhou. But he didn't know if he was the Zhuang Zhou who had dreamt he was a butterfly, or a butterfly dreaming that he was Zhuang Zhou. Between Zhuang Zhou and the butterfly, there must be some distinction! This is called the *Transformation of Things*.

The Butterfly Dream brings up some questions that are quite relevant to identity. How do we know if we are dreaming or awake? How do we know that this isn't a simulation? Is there a real self we can point to? This radical skepticism of selfhood has a long and storied philosophical history. David Hume used introspective awareness to also scrutinize the idea of personal identity:

> For my part, when I enter most intimately into what I call myself, I always stumble on some particular perception or other, of heat or cold, light or shade, love or hatred, pain or pleasure. I can never catch myself at any time without a perception, and can never observe anything but the perception. When my perceptions are removed for any time, as by sound sleep; so long am I insensible of myself, and may truly be said not to exist.

This directly reflects the Butterfly Dream, in which Zhuang Zhou ceased to exist as soon as he "became" the butterfly. It is perhaps only our perception that can bring us a sense of selfhood. And this perception is admittedly fraught with errors—such as mistaking one's dream for reality. This is also why Descartes could claim nothing more than "I think therefore I am." Only his ability to think—to reflect and experience his perceptions proves some sense of self. We could well be brains in a vat, characters in a dream, or NPCs in a video game. But at the very least, we appear to be bundles of perception that provide an illusion of self-hood.

If our identity is so frivolous, why do many of us become so obsessive over who we are? Where is an essential self? The *Zhuangzi* rejects the notion of a true self or original "I." Instead, the text endorses the preservation and utility of emptiness. The usefulness of a cup is found above all in its emptiness, in its ability to carry liquid.

Similarly, Taoist philosophy tends to value the free space that comes with not having this hidden true self. In sincerity, this free space is obstructed by social roles. In authenticity, it is blocked by an essential self. And in profilicity, it is encumbered largely by the audience—the general peer. When we obstruct this inner emptiness, we lose out on the ability to adapt, as demonstrated by Zhuangzi's story of the tree:

Carpenter Shih went to Ch'i, and when he got to Crooked Shaft, he saw a serrate oak standing by the village shrine. It was broad enough to shelter several thousand oxen and measured a hundred spans around, towering above the hills. The lowest branches were eighty feet from the ground, and a dozen or so of them could have been made into boats. There were so many sightseers that the place looked like a fair, but the carpenter didn't even glance around and went on his way without stopping. His apprentice stood staring for a long time and then ran after Carpenter Shih and said, "Since I first took up my ax and followed you, Master, I have never seen timber as beautiful as this. But you don't even bother to look, and go right on without stopping. Why is that?"

"Forget it—say no more!" said the carpenter. "It's a worthless tree! Make boats out of it, and they'd sink; make coffins, and they'd rot in no time; make vessels, and they'd break at once. Use it for doors, and it would sweat sap like pine; use it for posts, and the worms would eat them up. It's not a timber tree—there's nothing it can be used for. That's how it got to be that old!"

After Carpenter Shih had returned home, the oak tree appeared to him in a dream and said, "What are you comparing me with? Are you comparing me with those useful trees? The cherry apple, the pear, the orange, the citron, the rest of those fructiferous trees and shrubs—as soon as their fruit is ripe, they are torn apart and subjected to abuse. Their big limbs are broken off, their little limbs are yanked around. Their utility makes life miserable for them, and so they don't get to finish out the years Heaven gave them, but are cut off in mid-journey. They bring it on themselves—the pulling and tearing of the common mob. And it's the same way with all other things.

"As for me, I've been trying a long time to be of no use, and though I almost died, I've finally got it. This is of great use to me. If I had been of some use, would I ever have grown this large? Moreover, you and I are both of us things. What's the point of this—things condemning things? You, a worthless man about to die—how do you know I'm a worthless tree?"

The value of the tree was found in its emptiness—in its ability to momentarily accept without entirely succumbing to the values and beliefs around it. This allowed it to survive. Such an outlook on life reflects the common saying that "the true mark of intelligence is when someone can entertain an idea without accepting it." Here, we can alter it slightly: *The true mark of the adaptive individual is when someone can entertain an identity without becoming it.*

This is genuine pretending—an "existential sort of play" in which one takes on roles (whether that be an occupation, a social role, a family role, or pretty much anything) while retaining that inner emptiness. To return to the cup analogy, genuine pretending allows for the emptiness to return. How useful would a cup be if you could only fill it once? Taoism proposes that one should preserve the inner emptiness, the bundles of perception (we may call it consciousness), and adjust to external circumstances. It can be filled out, yes, but it must be emptied out repeatedly.

Pretending here can be seen as a sort of play. And who is better at play than children? Children might take on the role of a firefighter or ninja, and they may take this role very seriously. They take it on genuinely. But just as soon as the role is no longer useful—their mom calls them in for dinner, for example—they can just as easily (well, hopefully) drop the act and adjust. This is partially because kids do not have rigid forms of identity. They have yet to lay claim on who they are. However, as we age, this ability to adjust becomes more difficult as the way we see ourselves becomes hardened (remember, once again, Marcel's crispation).

Instead, genuine pretending, like child's play, allows for the taking on of roles while maintaining the ability to remain contingent and transient. We avoid Marcel's crispation. The genuine pretender can shift in and out of different identities and avoid becoming obsessive. They loosen themselves from the burden of an identity that may become outdated, dangerous, or, at the very least, distasteful. Genuine pretending might be the best form of "being" we have if we are to accept the claim that human nature is largely marked by our creative ability to become what we are not. It allows us to adapt and adjust, to survive a world of constant technological and environmental shifts. Why not lean into our adaptability?

We find, after a long inquiry into who we are, one possible answer: *The less we think we know about ourselves, the better.* This is because the more we think we know about ourselves, the more likely we have already fallen into the trap of obsessive overidentification. In *Ecce Homo*, Nietzsche reminds us that "to become what one is, one must not have the faintest idea of what one is." To protest too much or affirm too much in terms of who we are might crystallize us in a shell of self-condemnation. We may end up limiting ourselves. Self-knowledge, the journey of becoming oneself, is a process of constant failures, deaths, and rebirths. We will continually lose and find who we are. And perhaps the sooner we accept this cycle, the easier and more fruitful the journey will be.

So far, we have explored the composition of our identity, both its content and the process of making oneself. According to those such as Trilling, Luhman, and Moeller, these mechanisms of identity-making are far from stable. Rather, they have shifted throughout history, from a compulsion towards sincerity to a romantic embrace of authenticity and finally to an algorithmically informed emphasis on profile-building. Importantly, one pitfall of identity-building persists across all eras of creating one's identity: overidentification. To overly endorse your identity runs the risk of placing too many existential eggs in your basket. It is only within the flexibility and plasticity of genuine pretending where we may begin to find some sense of direction.

As long as we continue moving along and learn to view ourselves as verbs rather than nouns, we should find ourselves all the more able to adapt, subsist, survive, and maybe, just maybe, feel all right. But there is still work to be done. While we have somewhat answered who we are, a larger question remains: How much of a say do we have in all of this? Can we actually decide to be this or that? A sense of identity or selfhood denotes a subject—something that has volition and can act on intention. Do we have a choice in what we become? Are we actually free? Does free will even exist? What is freedom? And is it even worth it?

Part 3

Becoming Oneself

In this part, we explore the more fundamentally uncomfortable questions: Why do we even want to form an identity? And is such an identity achievable? Does free will exist? And what is the point of all of this if we're just going to die? Above all, is there a proper way to live?

Genuine pretending may take some time to get used to. As demonstrated, we have found ourselves, so far, to be an intricate assemblage of permeable features and labels—such as those of our race, gender, and personality. And we have made ourselves in relation with (and sometimes in spite of) society. While certainly leading us somewhere, these paths still fail to fully satisfy that feeling of existential security. In this grand attempt to answer who we are, we may find ourselves even further from ourselves than before! How can you simply be yourself? I look at my dog—an adorable labradoodle with boundless energy. There's no apparent soul-searching, no real discontent at an existential level. Instead, she sleeps, eats, and plays, with very little contemplation or reflection. I'm honestly pretty jealous. Instead of a happy-go-lucky puppy, I find myself as a largely socially constructed human body with the burden of forming an identity. I have been thrown in here against my will, and must now figure out exactly what it is that I am supposed to be doing. A simple question emerges. How am I supposed to live?

Chapter 17

Our Ultimate Goal

It seems fairly easy to be a dog. There's little self-doubt, let alone existential despair. Why are humans condemned to go through such misery in their attempt to understand how to live?

Aristotle saw this as an inherent trait of humans—an attribute that fundamentally distinguishes us from our animal brethren. Unlike animals, who can go throughout the day unquestionably and enthusiastically, we have the ability to discern various paths and compare which will be better than others. This is *logos*—the capacity to apply wisdom and rational contemplation to our everyday lives. Remember that we are conscious beings with minds that can understand ourselves and the world around us. This act of understanding is the execution of *logos*, and it fundamentally keeps us from the blissful ignorance of the spider, the frog, and the goat.

Logos allows us to understand and pick apart the correct course of action—that which will be useful or beneficial for us. And yes, it has given us a great deal of tools to survive and has even led to the creation of inventions like the McRib. But with great power comes great responsibility. Beneficial to what? Useful to what end? Unlike animals, who appear to be set in their ways through simply surviving and existing, humans appear to have much greater needs in terms of what they are aiming for while they are alive. What do we want out of this life? What is our purpose—our *telos* or aim? We will overthink ourselves into depression in an attempt to understand what we are to do with our lives. Simply being is not enough.

Aristotle elaborates further on his distinction between man and animal. All animals—including us—are nutritive. "Nutritive" is the essential "soul" or will of our biology, which strives for and is nourished by food, water, and shelter. And so every living creature has a nutritive soul, an inherent drive towards survival. Its aims are simple and generate little doubt over those who pursue it diligently. The mouse will pursue the cheese. The plant will stretch for its nourishing photons. And I will make sure to run inside when there is a hurricane. Existence, for the nutritive soul, is simple and, in the best of ways, animalistic.

As Aristotle continues, we also possess what he calls a *sensitive-locomotive soul*—a will that perceives and feels. This sensitive soul separates animals and humans from plants, as the former can perceive and experience the world around them to a degree that is at least measurable to the average observer. The dog will wag his tail when he sees his owner. I will blush when my crush says hello to me. This is a life of pleasure and pain—of sensation and nothing more.

Of course, a life ruled by the pursuit of pleasure and the avoidance of pain sounds fairly bare. For example, we appear to have a strong urge to form an identity, some sort of ontological vessel that assures and affirms our being through its outer representation in society *and* internal subjectivity. We will go through pain to do this—we will get tattoos, fight and die in wars, and force ourselves into jobs that we do not necessarily like in order to affirm this identity. To purely have a drive towards pleasure, at least basic pleasure, is to disregard a whole list of examples of us torturing ourselves for some self-clarification.

While utilitarians such as Jeremy Bentham championed this primacy of pleasure over pain as the ultimate aim of humanity, others have since questioned the philosophy of utilitarianism. Is the greatest pleasure for the greatest amount of people justifiable if we have to kill for it? If I had to kill a baby, but it assured the eternal happiness of eight people, would the utilitarian doctrine allow for it?

Here is another question. Are all pleasures experienced the same? Is laughing at an Adam Sandler movie of the same quality of pleasure as enjoying *Citizen Kane*? This is what John Stuart Mill meant by: *I would rather be Socrates sad than a pig happy.* Perhaps some delights are of a higher quality of delightfulness than others. And yes, there may be an inherent pretentiousness that defines our species.

Aristotle devised a third form of the soul in consideration of these higher aims—a soul that is solely possessed by humans (and perhaps, in a few years, artificial intelligence): *the rational soul.* This is where we apply *logos* and, hopefully, clarify what the aim of humans could be. For Aristotle, that is to live in accordance with reason. This will result in *eudaimonia*—"human flourishing" or "a meaningful life." To be eudaemonic is quite different from the pursuit of hedonia, the sort of life of pleasure (of hedonism) that the sensitive soul pursues. For better or worse, we are destined to overthink how exactly to flourish and live under the guise of reason.

Aristotle specifically answered this question—that is, he *very specifically answered this question*—in his treatise *Nicomachean Ethics*. This book proposes a series of specific virtues that one should live in accordance with, with each virtue corresponding to some level of moderation. For example, Aristotle argued that one should neither be too brazen nor too cowardly. Rather, they should live a life of proper courage, where they are reasonably brave in the face of danger. The good life, for Aristotle, is one of moderation derived through moral understanding and the formation of proper habit.

In short, we can apply Aristotle's notion of eudaimonia to explain our difficulty in simply being. Humans, according to him, just aren't cut out for sitting around and eating nuts. We need to strive for something—something that he declared to be the ultimate aim of our existence. This is to apply our reasoning. Simple. Sweet.

But there remains at least one issue.

Is anything about our existence reasonable to begin with? We are not only thrown into this world with a set of random and arbitrary markers of identity and resources (or limitations) that we will have to work with in order to achieve a good life. We are also thrown *out of it*, randomly and with no warning. We die. What is the point of living well if it all inevitably ends? We have no guarantee of an after-life. No reward for all of our logos-crafting. This is a terrible bargain. While we are rational beings with an assured sense of responsibility in terms of living good lives, the sinister presence of mortality perpetually lingers, asking us: *To what ends?*

Chapter 18

The Vital Lie of Character

Man has a symbolic identity that brings him sharply out of nature.
He is a symbolic self, a creature with a name, a life history...
This immense expansion, this dexterity...gives to man literally
the status of a small god in nature...Yet, at the same time, as the
Eastern sages also knew, man is a worm and food for worms.
This is the paradox; he is out of nature and hopelessly in it.

—Ernest Becker

And so we have landed right on the million-dollar question. How do we live in the face of all of this horrid meaninglessness? In the face of death? For many of us, it's easier to ignore the fact of our impending demise. After all, thinking about our eventual fate as worm food can be pretty anxiety-inducing. Recall our discussion of Ernest Becker and his theory of evil. As previously discussed, Becker believed that evil emerged from this need to deny our deaths and limitations. The awful behavior we use towards others is, in a sense, often a matter of quelling our own deep-rooted anxiety. This anxiety, Becker argues, stems from an existential paradox that is inherent to the human condition. We are so complicated and yearn to grow and realize our potentials, and yet we know it will all end.

This denial of death does not always require an unfortunate other through which we can dehumanize and punish as a means of quelling our own anxieties. We may also deny and punish aspects of ourselves in order to manage this existential paradox. How so? To cope, Becker argues, we deny our death and keep it in our unconscious. This is through the process of what Becker defines as "*the vital lie of character.*" We cannot accept the fact that we are helpless, that all of this appears for nothing—a cruel joke. Our character, our personality, is thus formed as a complex defense mechanism that allows us to feel safe and protected. Becker writes, "We repress our bodies to purchase a soul that time cannot destroy; we sacrifice pleasure to buy immortality; we encapsulate ourselves to avoid death. And life escapes us while we huddle within the defended fortress of character."

Becker suggests that many of us are currently living lives that are, in some sense, untrue to ourselves. We have embraced the vital lie of character out of fear—out of an attempt to deny the only certainty there is: our mortality. To deny death, we must deny who we are. This could be called "bad faith" under Sartrean terms—the idea that we are in some way restricting or reducing ourselves to an identity. Sartre uses the example of a café waiter to illustrate his point: "There is no doubt I am in a sense a café waiter—otherwise could I not just as well call myself a diplomat or reporter? But if I am one, this cannot be in the mode of being-in-itself. I am a waiter in the mode of being what I am not."

As Sartre argues, we tend to box ourselves into rigidly defined roles and thus lose out on some core authentic traits. This does not mean that Sartre is entirely rejecting social roles. Rather, like Becker, he is simply gesturing towards the sort of limitations that society can place on us as individuals. Recall the sort of crispation that Gabriel Marcel used to describe the thick outer shell of traits and roles we use to identify ourselves. It is this sort of overidentification—with gender, with careers, with aspects of our personality—that can lead us astray, into *bad faith*. Yes, you are a waiter. But you are not *just* a waiter.

Sartre and most existentialists would likely argue that you are much more than could ever be articulated, and so to limit oneself to this crispation, this vital lie of character, is one of the greatest existential tragedies. Note that this is not reflecting the sort of turn-of-the-century authenticity that Trilling had described. This is not some advocacy for an essential self or true "Me" that will be uncovered with enough soul-searching. Rather, many of the philosophers discussed see the self as that sort of Dasein—a temporal and dynamic being-in-this-world that is more of a process than a stable and unified self. Who we are instead is a constant process of becoming.

Chapter 19

The Dizziness of Freedom

That's good and all, but this does absolutely nothing for us in the sense of knowing where to go. Who do we become exactly? And it doesn't help that the existentialists rarely proposed any sort of ethics consistent with their dreadful analysis of the human condition. Sartre famously planned to write an ethics of existentialism and had even attached the movement to humanism and Marxism throughout his career.[†] But his project of forming an ethics of existentialism never fully came to be. Any example of what *good faith* would be in relation to *bad faith* is unfortunately restricted to a few vague footnotes. And Becker, an anthropologist more than a moral philosopher, only gestured towards the importance of art and faith in properly denying our deaths. He saw the crux of our dilemma—this existential freedom mixed in with the limitations of mortality—as something that would be incredibly difficult to work around for most. We are free to do what we want, *and* whatever we decide to do is pretty much meaningless in the grand scheme of things. It is all, in the end, quite arbitrary.

This was also of central concern to Soren Kierkegaard, who wrote an entire essay on the sort of anxiety that arises from acknowledgment of this fact. *The Concept of Anxiety*, written in 1844, explores our freedom in terms of a man at a cliff's edge who experiences a simultaneous aversion to falling and a peculiar desire to jump. The fact that we have the supposed freedom to do something self-destructive or wrong instills

---

† *The Ethics of Ambiguity*, by Simone de Beauvoir, is as close as we may ever get to an ethical philosophy of the existentialist tradition. It is a beautiful work that champions freedom, authenticity, and love as central aims of existentialist ethics.

in us some sense of anxiety and dread. In our state of becoming, we are confronted with seemingly endless possibilities. We could stay, or we could go. Kierkegaard describes this arbitrariness brilliantly:

> If you marry, you will regret it; if you do not marry, you will also regret it; if you marry or if you do not marry, you will regret both; whether you marry or you do not marry, you will regret both. Laugh at the world's follies, you will regret it; weep over them, you will also regret it; if you laugh at the world's follies or if you weep over them, you will regret both.

The infinite decisions we could make—and the underlying feeling that some are better than others—fill us with anguish. Yes, in *Nicomachean Ethics*, Aristotle offers some fairly direct answers to how one should act. But we can't just make a list of rules and guidelines for every possible decision. We are, in the view of Kierkegaard, unbearably free at every moment, condemned to be both sculpture and sculptor. To do so would be to claim that we could somehow predict the best course of action at all times. Our *logos* is not *that* great. We have an endless list of heuristics and cognitive biases that obfuscate our decision-making. Add to this dreadful situation the fact that time is always running out, and we can end up entirely paralyzed. There's a deadline! Sylvia Plath beautifully illustrates this sense of fleeting choice in *The Bell Jar*:

> I saw my life branching out before me like the green fig tree in the story. From the tip of every branch, like a fat purple fig, a wonderful future beckoned and winked. One fig was a husband and a happy home and children, and another fig was a famous poet and another fig was a brilliant professor, and another fig was Ee Gee, the amazing editor, and another fig was Europe and Africa and South America, and another fig was Constantin and Socrates and Attila and a pack of other lovers with queer names and offbeat professions, and another

fig was an Olympic lady crew champion, and beyond and above these figs were many more figs I couldn't quite make out. I saw myself sitting in the crotch of this fig tree, starving to death, just because I couldn't make up my mind which of the figs I would choose. I wanted each and every one of them, but choosing one meant losing all the rest, and, as I sat there, unable to decide, the figs began to wrinkle and go black, and, one by one, they plopped to the ground at my feet.

As Plath demonstrates, making the right choice is easier said than done. We often operate on a limited amount of information with no clear sense of what the future will hold. Yes, we can look towards certain philosophies as guiding lights in our deliberations. But these can only help us so much. Take the Aristotelian good life, based on virtue and moderation. Is it as easy as Aristotle suggested? To live virtuously? Does a life of *logos* and moderation quell this underlying sense of finitude? We are starving to death at the crotch of this fig tree, unable to choose which path is the most eudaemonic.

A career in finance. A new partner. Opening up an NGO. Who is to say what is the correct answer to the problem of existence, especially when each individual has their own particular proclivities and inclinations? Nowadays, with so much information and a collision of cultural exchange that has cast many claims on what is universally "true" or "virtuous" as largely relative and localized, it can feel like there are endless opportunities with no clear sense of which is the right one. We could invest in the wrong relationship, career, or stock. We could waste our precious time on the wrong things. So what is the right thing to do? What does that even mean? Perhaps we are getting ahead of ourselves. I think a better question—one that could provide us with some more philosophical fun (and thus less clear answers)—is whether we can do anything at all.

Chapter 20

Free Will

Throughout this book, we have assured ourselves of the existential fact that we are condemned to be free. This is, after all, the source of your misery, your crisis. You have come to a point in your life where everything is up in the air—who you are, who you could be, and everything around you. All fleeting elements are forged through the indifferent gods of facticity and contingency. Do we have any freedom in this?

To be an individual with a set identity—that is, a *subject*—often implies some agent of intentionality that you could point to as a source of selfhood. We do not simply experience ourselves as a bundle of perceptions that passively receive the world around us. We also experience the *self* as a source of volitional behavior. In other words, we not only experience the self but we also, on top of that, believe that we have some say in what this self can do. We are not just something to be experienced. We are a process to be undertaken. How this is undertaken, presumably, is up to us. As we are thrown into existence, we realize that we are burdened with this sense of self as something we are responsible for. This is our freedom of will—the liberty and responsibility we possess in willing ourselves in one direction or another.

Nietzsche illustrates the strangeness of this situation in his exploration of free will. To will something implies command over something thought to obey us (i.e., our will). Freedom of will, he explains further, is a function of willing something in oneself that will obey our command. From this, some sort of action is executed. Once acted out, the commander of the will (the subject) rejoices in executing the task.

And so commander and executor become one. We see ourselves as both the initiator and initiated.

For example, I might wish to go to the beach. I have a vision in my head of splashing in the waves and reading a good book. Maybe I'm meeting a friend there. Whatever the case, I have some motivation or drive that represents "me" in some way. Perhaps under sincerity, it fills my social role as a beach-goer. Or, under authenticity, it might be an act of rebellion against going to a class or seminar that I am compelled to attend. "No," I say. My true self belongs outside of the classroom, and instead, I should live authentically before the great ocean and among the seabirds. And even under profilicity, I might simply presume that being able to take a selfie at the beach could provide some exhibition value for my Instagram. Perhaps I can temporarily act out the role of an influencer and, for a few hours, bask in the glow of digital hearts and smiles. No matter the reasoning behind it, I now must command myself—will myself—to the beach. I have fixed my will exclusively on doing one thing and one thing only. And once there, I have successfully "willed freely."

But it should be noted that this sort of "freedom"—the point of agency—occurred just before I grabbed my car keys and swimming trunks and arrived at the beach. Once set in motion, my will was constrained to a specific objective. The "magic" of this sort of freedom came at the moment of choice—in which I wondered what I should do with my day. There I was "free." Once initiated, however, I moved from a state of being free from influence—of deliberating and contemplating my course of action—to a state of being free *to go* to the beach.

The Two Liberties

Is the mere absence of external (and internal) constraints enough to define freedom? This discussion tiptoes along one of the most useful attempts at defining liberty, that by philosopher Isaiah Berlin. Liberty, here, can be seen as a more specific form of freedom—one that is often evoked in reference to the rights of political groups. You would be hard-pressed to find someone against liberty nowadays. The concept itself denotes some sort of goodness—the ability to be creative, authentic, and act on one's own intentions. How nice! But we might not always be talking about the same sort of freedom. According to Berlin, liberty can be categorized into two types: *positive and negative liberty*.

Negative liberty is the one most of us will be familiar with. It's simply defined as the absence of obstacles and constraints. It implies the total freedom of action—the capacity to freely decide among a set of available choices. In Berlin's words, negative liberty answers the question: "What is the area within which the subject—a person or group of persons—is or should be left to do or be what he is able to do or be, without interference by other persons?"

Negative freedom is unconstrained, non-coerced, and seemingly limitless. But recall Nietzsche's concern about free will. Who is commanding the will? Who is the commander of our compulsions—the source of volition? And why are we compelled to follow them? Here, Berlin describes positive liberty: What, or who, is the source of control or interference that can determine someone to do, or be, this rather than that?

Well, this type of freedom doesn't sound very…freeing, no? Whereas one implies the absence of constraints, the other suggests the addition of something for freedom to occur. While negative liberty is easier to theorize over—as simply the absence of external constraints—positive liberty requires us to make certain claims when someone is considered to be acting freely. Where negative liberty is *freedom from*, positive liberty is the *freedom to*. It implies something beyond negativity or mere independence.

This is where we get into murky ethical waters. A friend who is living "freely" by drinking constantly, eating potato chips, and playing video games may consider themselves to be acting undeniably out of freedom. However, you, the concerned friend, may instead suggest that they are a slave to their impulses and appetites—that they are not being true to their higher selves. You may hold a higher opinion of your friend than he does. But is this fair? Aren't you infringing on his negative liberty to eat Cheetos?

The addict is another splendid case study for positive liberty. They often have the freedom from constraints that would allow them to carry out their addiction. They have, for example, the time and money to abuse alcohol and drugs—or at least they find the time and money to do so. But would we suggest that the freedom *to* pursue these "hobbies" is that which composes a noble and dignified life? Here, we find ourselves presented with some presumptions over what makes a truly "free" individual. For example, we might claim that a free individual is someone who does not rely on substances. But doesn't our attempt to define the characteristics of a truly free individual limit their own negative liberty in some way? We presume that with the privilege of negative freedom—the space and time we are given to make our own decisions—that there is an equal responsibility to use it correctly.

This is a prominent existential theme: that with freedom comes responsibility. Of course, this tends to also instill anxiety. As Soren Kierkegaard famously wrote, "Anxiety is the dizziness of freedom." We suddenly feel thrown into the world, with little rhyme or reason, and find ourselves compelled to make with our lives what we can. But what exactly is the right way to go about things? What are we free to do? Yes, negative liberty affords us the ability to fulfill our potential or, at the very least, to explore our own preferences. But what is this potential? What are these preferences?

In the form of positive liberty, freedom can feel like a burden. This can come in the form of that Sunday evening dread, where we find ourselves bored and despondent, grasping for any semblance of a plan or activity. At its worst, it can develop into an existential crisis. We become privy to a certain arbitrariness that underlies all of our decisions. There is no right or wrong choice. We are entirely free. But free to do what exactly? We feel the full weight of our freedom—that everything is on the table. And so many of us turn to things that will limit this sense of endless opportunity—through drugs, alcohol, sex, and menial entertainment. These are far more appealing options than actually sitting down and reflecting on who we are and who we would like to be.

The Paradox of Freedom

Psychologist Erich Fromm reflected on this question in his work *Escape from Freedom.* In it, he asked an important question: "Can freedom become a burden too heavy for man to bear, something he tries to escape from? Why then is it that freedom is for many a cherished goal and for others a threat? Is there not also, perhaps, besides an innate desire for freedom, an instinctive wish for submission?"

For Fromm, freedom is an ambiguous gift. Negative liberty has allowed for the emergence of the *individual*—an unencumbered and free human being who can (supposedly) choose their own course of action and lifestyle. They are no longer entirely bound to the primary ties of the church, the state, or the sorts of cultural expectations that are inherent to the Age of Sincerity. The individual is fundamentally a product of the Age of Authenticity—championing independence and sovereignty above all else.

Yet as Fromm notes, this has also led to an intolerable and existentially nightmarish sense of isolation and confusion. The modern individual is fundamentally alone because of their freedom. They can live quite easily with no attachments or connections. I'm sure you have heard of those poor souls who pass away in their single-bed apartments only to be found months later when the power company inevitably checks in on them. Such individuals lived lives of quiet independence, free from the imposition of loved ones and friends. While they were free from social constraints, we must ask ourselves if such individuals were free to live out the sort of existence that a human being would consider to be *good*. Fromm points out this lag between negative and positive liberty and its horrific consequences: "The result of this disproportion between freedom from any tie and the lack of possibilities for the positive realization of freedom and individuality has led, in Europe, to a panicky flight from freedom into new ties or at least complete indifference."

Fromm saw this resistance we possessed towards freedom manifest, at its worst, in the totalitarianism that persisted throughout the twentieth century. He thought that the citizens of Russia and Germany, for example, looked to a higher power in the form of a strong leader. This was an attempt to escape their own burden of freedom through believing in and serving a seemingly stable ideology—no matter how nightmarish it might be. Isaiah Berlin, interestingly enough, also developed his concept of the two liberties during the Cold War, a period of time characterized by such totalitarianism. This era was often marked by dictators and autocrats who would mobilize their populations by means of declaring what was considered to be *good*. They would utilize positive liberty to justify their monstrous atrocities by convincing their population of their own notion of freedom. Censorship, extrajudicial killings, invasions. These were, after all, justified in the name of freedom. You are free to serve the state, the proletariat, the Motherland. Just look at the words of Stalin as he used the threat of losing independence (that is, freedom) as an excuse for his Five-Year Plan, which would result in the deaths of an estimated six to seven million people:

> To slacken the tempo would mean falling behind. And those who fall behind get beaten. But we do not want to be beaten. No, we refuse to be beaten!…Such is the law of the exploiters—to beat the backward and the weak. It is the jungle law of capitalism. You are backward, you are weak—therefore you are wrong; hence you can be beaten and enslaved. You are mighty—therefore you are right; hence we must be wary of you. That is why we must no longer lag behind. In

the past we had no fatherland, nor could we have had one. But now that we have overthrown capitalism and power is in our hands, in the hands of the people, we have a fatherland, and we will uphold its independence. Do you want our socialist fatherland to be beaten and to lose its independence?

Here we see Stalin referring to a period of control and domination that had resulted in the oppression of Russia. According to his narrative, the collective desire to overcome such a historical pattern must be achieved by any means necessary. Of course, mythologies of emancipation, such as the one above, ironically resulted in some of the worst atrocities committed by human beings. As Berlin noted, positive liberty soon became a source of control and constraint. Those who backed genocidal regimes were seduced by the idea that one's striving towards freedom was no longer an individual journey. Instead, it was fully aligned with the collective goal of the nation, the Proletariat, or the Reich. As Berlin wrote:

> Once I take this view, I am in a position to ignore the actual wishes of men or societies, to bully, oppress, torture in the name, and on behalf, of their "real" selves, in the secure knowledge that whatever is the true goal of man…must be identical with his freedom.

By taking on this view, the individual no longer had to go through the trouble of determining how they should live. This was now outsourced to a larger collective—a movement that would result in the deaths of millions around the globe.

Chapter 21

The Myth of Self-Improvement

The irony here is self-evident; freedom can be used to oppress and restrain. And this is just as evident now as it was then. Thinkers such as Byung-Chul Han still warn against the supposed freedoms we have been blessed with and the narratives spun to support them. He argues that neoliberalism uses our feelings of freedom to produce more capital. It is this feeling of freedom that becomes an effective means of self-exploitation. It is as if we have gained the freedom to whip ourselves. Han writes:

> The disappearance of domination does not entail freedom. Instead, it makes freedom and constraint coincide. Thus, the achievement subject gives itself over to compulsive freedom—that is, to the free constraint of maximizing achievement. Excess work and performance escalate into auto-exploitation.

Han goes further and claims that we do not really freely work towards our own needs. Rather, we serve the "needs" of capital—the need for capital to circulate, propagate, and expand its territory. In a disturbing analogy, Han likens humans—that is, workers and consumers (all in one)—to the "genital organs" of capital. Yes, the entrepreneur believes they are a project that can be fashioned freely into whatever they like. But this is a means to an end. Han writes, "The freedom of capital achieves self-realization by way of individual freedom." Anything that represents freedom—emotionality, play, communication—are denigrated to exploitation by capital. They are seen instead as worthy sources of revenue. Sure, we are free from a whole host of constraints, and so negative liberty is satisfied. And we are free to become our authentic selves. But this authenticity is specifically tied to marketability and commodifying ourselves. This is the nefarious character of positive liberty under capitalism. We have come to view ourselves as a failing project that is persistently unable to fulfill the standards of self-improvement.

And the entrepreneur experiences tremendous guilt if they do fail in this project—this goal of self-realization or self-actualization. Han brilliantly argues that this has led to an internalization of class struggle. The master and slave have become one. We are the commodity and the commodified, the elite and the proletariat. Han further describes this process as *auto-exploitation*, where we push ourselves to do more, be more, and become more. Instead of aggression towards some outside force of oppression, we turn it inwards. And this becomes depression. This is our present state. We find ourselves free to post whatever, Uber Eats whatever, and live wherever. And under all this is an underlying pressure to maximize ourselves, sometimes resulting in considerable sadness and despair.

For Han, the positive liberty of neoliberalism isn't so far off from that of the totalitarian horrors of the twentieth century that Berlin warned against. Whereas the citizens of Nazi Germany may have mistaken the needs of Hitler with the needs of their own, we now have mistaken the needs of capital as belonging to us. We are *free*—to make money. And to make money, one must "self-realize" in the most marketable of ways. This is perhaps another indication of the relative utility of proficility over authenticity. Whereas authenticity requires one to follow an original self, regardless of marketability, proficility simply urges us to select whatever is most commodifiable and thus conducive to the needs of capital. In the words of Gabor Maté:

> We are steeped in the normalized myth that we are, each of us, mere individuals striving to attain private goals. The more we define our-

selves that way, the more estranged we become from vital aspects of who we are and what we need to be healthy.

Psychology has extensively researched the effects of this auto-exploitation, which is often called *alienation* in Marxist literature. It is a dislocation from who we are, the instrumentalization of ourselves in the service of capital. And nefariously, unlike previous forms of rule, it uses the very sense of freedom as a means of power. We identify our own goals with the goals of profit and investment. Psychologist Tim Kasser defines self-interest, a desire for financial success, high levels of consumption, and a competitive relational style as the four principles of American Corporate Capitalism, evidently internalized by many as values of their own. Is this not positive liberty at its most destructive? To have convinced ourselves that we are acting freely when, in fact, we are subordinate to the external forces of corporate capitalism? As if we ever had any choice. Our compulsion to improve emerges from the struggle to survive under capitalism.

Chapter 22

The Will to Survive

Positive liberty brings us back to the issue of authenticity—is there really some sort of volitional self or commander of our will that we could refer to make the "right" decision? In simple terms, how do we know when we are acting freely? How do we know when we have our "best" interests at heart? Perhaps this is never truly up to us. Maybe, just maybe, all of that anxiety we experience over our freedom is just wasted energy. What if there is no commander that wills our will? What if we were never truly free? Hard determinism, the belief that everything we do is predetermined by the natural laws of physics and chemistry, suggests that there is no free will. To be paranoid about mistakenly serving the goals of some totalitarian leader, an addiction, or capital is to waste our time. Perhaps we will never be truly free. The authentically independent self could simply be an illusion as we are at all times moved along by the same principles of causation. Everything is predetermined.

A more philosophical example of determinism can be found in the pessimism of Arthur Schopenhauer, who suggested that the will runs all actions and behaviors. Schopenhauer first looks at what we could call negative liberty through his examination of physical freedom, which is simply the absence of apparent external constraints, like hand-cuffs (unless, of course, you are into that). Well, this is commonly seen as a clear and undeniable state of freedom. You are, for example, free to move your hand. And you are free to not be imprisoned. You are, by all accounts, unconstrained and free to do as you wish. But what do you wish to do? Who is the wisher of these wishes? Schopenhauer cites a serious problem that is reminiscent of Nietzsche's own enquiry between the commander of the will and the will itself. If the will is free, what is it free to do? Well, it is free to will what it is free to will. But what if the will wishes to do other than what it has willed? Can one will what one willed to will? Is there freedom in this willing? How much agency do we actually have over our own will? Schopenhauer illustrates this point further:

> I can do what I will: I can, if I will, give everything I have to the poor and thus become poor myself—if I will! But I cannot will this, because the opposing motives have much too much power over me for me to be able to. On the other hand, if I had a different character, even to the extent that I were a saint, then I would be able to will it. But then I could not keep from willing it, and hence I would have to do so.

Do we have any say regarding what we desire or will? All of this talk of willing this and willing that points to a central concept in Schopenhauer's idea of reality itself: *the will*. This will, a simple blind desire for preservation and survival, is the fuel that drives motion in the universe, according to Schopenhauer. In a sense, Schopenhauer's will shares similarities with Aristotle's sensory-locomotive soul. This primal drive grows plants, draws magnets together, and compels us to fall in love. It is everything and everywhere. And Schopenhauer, being the hardcore naturalist that he is, sees it as a fairly unintelligent drive—one that is relentless in its attempt to satisfy its needs. The will could be equated to the hard determinist's own idea of natural laws—it isn't necessarily serving some higher purpose. Rather, it simply strives for its own maintenance and sustenance. From this, Schopenhauer takes a stance similar to Buddhism's take on desire: The will is the root of our suffering. Our lives are largely characterized by the striving to fulfill this will. In this sense, we are not entirely free. We are instead always operating on behalf of our will in terms of surviving and maintaining our homeostasis.

This perspective on free will is reminiscent of some present-day hard determinists, such as the primatologist Robert Sapolsky, who considers all human behavior to be primarily emerging from endocrinal and neuronal predeterminants. In Sapolsky's latest book, *Determined: A Science of Life Without Free Will*, he makes the basic claim that we are entirely absent of free will. The simple feeling that one had some intention and was in some sense aware of alternative decisions is just that—a feeling. We do not control our actions. Rather, they are the product of an ongoing historical process of causal factors that we never had any control over. He argues that for some sort of free will to exist, it would have to function independently from our biology or the environment for it to be proved. This would be observable—perhaps at the neuronal level. Instead, Sapolsky notes that pretty much all of our behavior can be accounted for in terms of this blind drive towards survival and homeostasis.

Although Schopenhauer existed at a time in which science struggled to account for much of our lived experience, his concept of the will seems to hold up here, at least in relation to the ideas of determinists such as Sapolsky. We are machines programmed to survive, and much of this survival is fueled by a psychological desire. In simple terms, Schopenhauer claims (and Sapolsky would likely agree) that we are doing what we will at all times. We are our will. So, both negative liberty and positive liberty are simply illusions or myths. There is no absence of external or internal constraints because there is nothing to constrain.

One small issue. Why do we often risk our own survival—our own homeostasis—to achieve certain goals? We start wars. We surf in shark-infested territory. We go skydiving. We fall in obsessive love with people who might not have our best interests at heart. A myriad of examples throw into question the extent to which we are truly following this blind desire to survive. Wouldn't these risky behaviors go against Schopenhauer's will in some way? Don't these activities jeopardize our security and basic physiological needs? What exactly are people getting out of this?

Chapter 23

Flow

Recall Aristotle's argument that humans are capable of experiencing far more than mere pleasure and pain. Although Schopenhauer's will (and Sapolsky's biological determinism) paints a simple picture of human emotion ranging from pain to pleasure, the seemingly irrational and, at times, uncomfortable activities we are drawn towards suggest that Aristotle was correct. We crave something more. This phenomenon was investigated by Mihaly Csikszentmihalyi, a Hungarian American psychologist, who was interested in the motivations behind those who regularly engage in risky hobbies like windsurfing and rock climbing.

Firstly, Csikszentmihalyi made the crucial distinction between pleasure and enjoyment. Whereas pleasure calms our need for satiation and satisfies our more biologically programmed desires, enjoyment provides a sense of complexity and transcendence. Just look back on your own life. When were you most happy? Surely, there's a vast list of tasty food and pleasurable intimate moments you could replay in your head. But it's just as likely that you cherish a wide range of far more *meaningful* experiences—conversations with friends, getting through a difficult book, finalizing a project, and learning to skateboard. When you look back on these memories, you might not have a clear memory of pure pleasure or comfort. In fact, you might remember them with a great deal of discomfort and anxiety. And yet these could be seen as some of the most enjoyable moments of your life. It is as if time flew by, and you completely lost yourself in the task at hand. This is what Csikszentmihalyi calls *flow*, a concept that he would eventually develop into an entire psychological field called *flow psychology*.

This distinction between pleasure and enjoyment is at the root of the work of flow psychology. Csikszentmihalyi describes it as "the science of the mental state of operation in which a person performing an activity is fully immersed in a feeling of energized focus and enjoyment." Flow is what we experience when we enjoy a certain activity. Time flies. You stop thinking about yourself so much. And you find your focus entirely consumed on the task at hand. Csikszentmihalyi makes the argument that those activities in which we derive mere pleasure—TV, fast food, gambling—are activities that do not reflect the sort of agency that is possible for human beings. We become prisoners to our pleasures, to the sort of biological will of Schopenhauer's philosophy. Pleasure, for one, involves little regard for what we genuinely want to do. Dangerously, it masks itself under the guise of liberation. Of course, giving into our genetic programming when we are hungry or when we desire sex is, in a sense, "freeing." Nevertheless, one can equally make the case that giving in is to become a slave to your urges. Csikszentmihalyi writes:

> The only authority many people trust today is instinct. If something feels good, if it is natural and spontaneous, then it must be right. But when we follow the suggestions of genetic and social instructions without question we relinquish the control of consciousness and become helpless playthings of impersonal forces.

This sort of critique of modernity suggests that we rarely make time for enjoyment nowadays and instead follow our impulses without regard. In other words, we tend to prioritize pleasure over enjoyment. Pornography, fast food, and the constant stimulation of social media all serve to keep us entirely fixated on satisfying our most basic needs. However, as Csikszentmihalyi argues, following these impulses minimizes our autonomy. We become less in control of our lives. Flow psychology advocates for a reclamation of our leisure time—into activities that promote more enjoyment and less pleasure. In pursuing flow activities, we can (we hope) reclaim a sense of who we are. So, what is the anatomy of such activities?

1. *Challenging activity that requires skill*
   Unlike watching television, the activity should push your abilities and make you feel effortful. How great it feels to execute your well-honed talents perfectly! Maybe it's learning a challenging piece on the piano or playing pick-up basketball with some well-skilled opponents. Note that this activity shouldn't greatly exceed your skill set nor make you feel bored from a lack of challenge. Thankfully, this aspect can be easily measured by your level of boredom or frustration. This characteristic of a flow activity is reminiscent of Soviet psychologist Lee Vygotsky's own concept of the *zone of proximal development*—in which he found that learning was most efficient in between the space where a child could do something entirely on their own and where they couldn't do something without assistance. This could be translated to finding an activity that promotes flow—where one is neither bored nor overwhelmed. It usually means an activity is just difficult enough to be challenging and might require some initial assistance.

2. *Merges action and awareness*
   Once completely absorbed in an activity, your actions may feel automatic. Your mind no longer wanders, and each move feels seemingly effortless (hence the term *flow*). Csikszentmihalyi writes, "In normal life, we keep interrupting what we do with doubts and questions…But in the flow there is no need to reflect because the action carries us forward as if by magic." This is evident when star athletes say they feel like the ball or hockey stick is merely an extension of themselves. They feel entirely at one with their activity.

3. *Clear goals and feedback*

Of course, you should be able to tell if the choices that you're making are the right ones. For instance, the hockey player knows what to do overall—to win the game as well as the assortment of smaller challenges that lead up to this. She may have to pass the puck to her teammate successfully and will know if she performed this well almost immediately. Or she may have to prevent an opponent from scoring on a breakaway and will rely on similar immediate feedback. Equally, the well-trained musician gets feedback at every chord and will have to readjust when something just doesn't feel right. Hence, feedback implies that there is a chance for error and improvement. This is certainly a characteristic absent when one marathons through *Seinfeld* over the weekend.

4. *Concentration*

This immersion should come from intense focus and concentration. In an almost monk-like trance, you lose any sense of self-consciousness. No longer are you preoccupied with the thoughts of what your hair looks like or what that guy or girl you have a crush on really thinks about you. Instead, every action is automatic. Csikszentmihalyi quotes one rock climber who beautifully describes this sort of egoless focus: "You are so involved in what you are doing (that) you aren't thinking of yourself as separate from the immediate activity…You don't see yourself as separate from what you are doing."

5. *The loss of self-consciousness*

Csikszentmihalyi writes, "The loss of the sense of a self separate from the world around it is sometimes accompanied by a feeling of union with the environment." As stated before, the concentration required for flow activities launches one into a state of automatic, unselfconscious operation. There is simply no room for self-scrutiny. We are vulnerable creatures, and for most of the day our doubts and anxieties interrupt our ability to focus and enjoy the moment at hand. Hence, entering into this sort of state is refreshing and emerges as one of the few moments of lucidity we truly experience throughout our lives.

6. *Alteration of time*

Finally, if you've ever played some sort of enjoyable game, you may have realized that time speeds up significantly. Strangely, one may feel that the clock moves faster, yet time has slowed down simultaneously. Professional athletes may feel as if they are operating in slow motion as they dodge and weave through opponents. However, they may also come out of the game asking themselves, "How is it already six p.m.?" Similarly, think back to those heated discussions with friends and family, where everyone is cued in and intensely focused on coming to a common truth or defending their position. The clock may have seemed to speed up throughout this conversation. Although this element of the flow may simply be a byproduct rather than a contributor to the overall positive experience itself, it does help us in our search for our own flow activities.

Csikszentmihalyi claims that activities involving this loss of self, time alteration, and clear feedback (among other elements) are truly free activities. They are activities done for themselves rather than to serve some sort of blind biological will. Viewing art, challenging oneself, setting out in nature. Such flow activities suggest that humans do desire something beyond mere pleasure and are willing to subject themselves to some level of discomfort in order to get to this. Why does simply watching TV or scrolling on your phone not reflect the image of a good life? Simply put, it is a life characterized by pleasure rather than enjoyment.

Chapter 24

Self-Complexity

What is so rewarding about flow activities? Flow psychologists such as Csikszentmihalyi believe that what is at the core of the sort of meaningful enjoyment one experiences in a state of flow is its ability to offer opportunities for *self-growth* through an interaction with unpredictable and spontaneous variables. They posit that it is because flow activities go beyond simply satisfying certain predictable needs that are already hardwired into us, such as hunger or thirst, that we find these activities to be far more enjoyable than they are merely pleasant. Eating a burger will, predictably, result in us feeling some pleasure. We have satisfied the need for hunger. In other words, we can anticipate the extent of the activity. Nothing about this activity will result in any sort of growth or renewed sense of self (unless, of course, it is a really good burger). But when we enter a chess match or take on a difficult math problem, we work with unknown variables. We encounter new obstacles that challenge our own capabilities, and so we are forced to react spontaneously. Through this, we discover new abilities and capabilities, as well as limitations in terms of who we are. Flow psychology settled on the fact that such activities are rewarding because we can *discover* more about ourselves and the world as a result of this engagement. It complexifies ourselves and our relationship with the world around us.

For example, if you are just getting into jazz, you might initially find little joy in the activity. However, as you find yourself exposed to different melodies and different jazz figures and begin reading up on specific movements, you encounter previously unknown information units. In doing so, you expand your own knowledge and perspective.

This also explains why flow requires the constant enhancement of challenges—because once we have discovered something new, it has been engaged with and internalized into who we are. Now, we need to discover more. The process of engaging in flow activities results in heightened *self-complexity*.

Why is this encounter with novel and unpredictable outcomes so enjoyable? As flow psychologists suggest, the desire to engage in these activities could be seen as an opportunity to increase our self-complexity—or expand ourselves in some manner. It is a natural impulse—to unfold ourselves through action and activity. This is reflected in the words of the poet Dante: "In every action…the main intention of the agent is to express his own image; thus it is that every agent, whenever he acts, enjoys the action. Because everything that exists desired to be, and by acting the agent unfolds his being, action is naturally enjoyable."

With flow activity, we enhance our complexity. But why do we need to increase self-complexity? The idea of complexity as beneficial has a certain evolutionary significance. Darwin did not use the phrase "the survival of the fittest" to refer to the strongest or most muscular. Rather, by fittest, he meant the most capable of adapting. Natural selection comes through an interaction between genes and the environment—with the genes that are most capable of surviving and reproducing being seen as the fittest.[†] But to survive, one must be able to adjust and adapt, as the environment is in constant flux. One guaranteed way to adapt is through increasing complexity. Increasing our skill set and expanding our knowledge of ourselves and the world will likely result in better reproductive fitness.

And perhaps humans are some of the best-suited organisms for such a task. An animal of limitless transgression with an incredulity

---

† One should always be wary here, as evolutionary psychology is a field fraught with logical issues. For one, the sociobiological fallacy suggests that evolutionary theory overemphasizes reproductive fitness as a driver of selection and ignores the cultural nuances of how we reward and punish different behavioral patterns in society.

towards definition. Our history is one of endless torment, a clash of claims over who we are with seemingly no solid footing. It is this persistent tension to seek some clarity over ourselves perpetually and then, when attained, the need to go beyond it. Perhaps this is why the project of defining human nature has filled so many philosophical and scientific texts with little consensus. In the words of Albert Camus, "Man is always a creature who refuses to be what he is."

This drive towards self-complexity is seemingly coded in our genes. We seek novelty and challenge and, in doing so, expand our skills and knowledge. Sapolsky even argues that this is the basis of our genetics: "What human genes are about, most dramatically, is coding for ways in which you have freedom from the effects of genetics" (2010). Our genes are constantly trying to outdo themselves. Flow is perhaps the process and reward of what we are genetically programmed to do in terms of evolutionary survival: to reach increasingly new levels of self-complexity. This was to become the basis of Csikszentmihalyi's theory behind the evolutionary function of flow. He writes:

> In order to ensure their own continuation, evolutionary processes seem to have built into our nervous systems a preference for complexity. Just as we experience pleasure when we do things that are necessary for survival, as we do when we eat or have sex, so, too do we experience enjoyment when we take on a project that stretches our skills in new directions, when we recognize and master new challenges. Every human being has this creative urge as his or her birthright. It can be squelched and corrupted, but it cannot be completely extinguished.

So flow feels rewarding because it is a direct engagement with something that simultaneously offers us respite from the constant struggle to survive *and* the capacity to become increasingly more complex (or, in Darwinian terms, *fit*). Schopenhauer, interestingly enough, did not see an engagement with such activities as forms of self-expansion. Rather, such activities and experiences offered little more than respite for him. While Schopenhauer did argue that the will is this aimless desire to survive and live, he also thought that *aesthetic experience*, an honest and present engagement with art, beauty, and culture, could help us escape from this enslavement to a cycle of pain and pleasure. Schopenhauer appreciated the arts for their capacity to offer us mental respite from the world's harshness.

Interestingly, he also posited that forms of art, such as music, were direct expressions of the very will that caused this harshness. Perhaps we could say something similar about flow activities here. However, he would likely not argue that such aesthetic experiences were leading to some greater version of ourselves. They were forms of escape above all else.

Chapter 25

The Will to Power

What if Schopenhauer failed to consider that part of the will to life—this struggle for homeostasis—involved increasing self-complexity and growth? This was a critique taken up by Nietzsche, who had been a former Schopenhauer fan-boy up until this point of contention. Nietzsche initially agreed with Schopenhauer's notion of the will and similarly saw the world as a dark, cruel space of pain and pleasure. However, with time, Nietzsche grew increasingly critical of this sort of negative view of the will and life itself. Perhaps there is some good that can come from life. Is it all just about survival and maintenance? Or are there some higher enjoyments, if you will, that make life worth living? And perhaps most importantly, are these enjoyments actually coherent with some sort of will or desire—rather than simply forms of escape as Schopenhauer would suggest? Nietzsche shared Csikszentmihalyi's curiosity in asking, *Why do we sometimes do things that seemingly go against our will?* Here is his explanation, as written in his work *Beyond Good and Evil*:

> Physiologists should think before putting down the instinct of self-preservation as the cardinal instinct of an organic being. A living thing seeks above all to discharge its strength—life itself is will to power; self-preservation is only one of the indirect and most frequent results.

What Nietzsche offers with this "will to power" is something that is lacking in Schopenhauer's theory. Like Schopenhauer's will to life, the will to power is about survival. But part of survival, according to Nietzsche and Csikszentmihalyi, is self-expansion and the desire to unfold one's being through activity. And so the will to power goes above and beyond the simple avoidance and aversion to death. In fact, it often leads to organisms willingly endangering their own lives in pursuit of growth and expansion! In Nietzsche's view, the desire we have for power is often greater than the desire we have to live. And this is because of the promise of self-expansion. Through expanding ourselves, we can become more powerful and thus capable of surviving. We become more evolutionarily capable of reproducing by increasing our self-complexity—challenging ourselves, creating art, growing and building, and developing.

Nietzsche, like Schopenhauer, is also skeptical of the notion of any freedom of will. This might surprise some, as he is often lumped in with other freedom-loving (or, at the very least, freedom-believing) existentialists such as Sartre and Kierkegaard. But it is important to note that Nietzsche's will to power is nonetheless a refined form of Schopenhauer's will to life. It is a blind impulse that informs our behavior. And so any sense of freedom we have is likely an illusion, carried along by a series of competing drives and desires. The mix of drives within us—guilt, anger, passion—fight it out. Sometimes one wins over another. Your desire to go play basketball, for example, might fight against your desire to call your mother. Neither choice is necessarily representative of a more authentic or free version of who you are. Each comes with its own strengths and weaknesses. According to Nietzsche, both drives will fight it out, and the strongest will reign supreme.

So are we entirely beholden to our desires—to the strongest of our wills? While both Schopenhauer and Nietzsche were skeptical of true freedom or agency, it should be noted that each had an idea of what one should do with regard to one's will. That is to say, each thinker at least proposed potential pathways towards living well on the chance that such freedom existed. Schopenhauer, viewing life as a tortuous cycle of suffering and torment, advocated for asceticism—the relinquishment of attachment. He reflected on the Buddhist approach—the cessation of desire as a strategy for minimizing our suffering. Yes, he suggested that time spent with art and beautiful things is, of course, quite pleasant and can even offer an escape from our existential pain. Still, overall, Schopenhauer advocated for a life of meager and monk-like living. While he maintained that such a lifestyle would be difficult for many—such as those in the West—he felt that this approach was the closest one could get to a good life.

Nietzsche rejected this wholeheartedly negative view of existence and instead proposed a life-affirming philosophy of overcoming. He believed that all of these drives within us, fighting and struggling in an attempt to reach some sort of greater self-expansion, could be unified into a single aim or goal. This harmony or coherence of wills would then lead to a good life—in which one lives in accordance with their own values and motivations. He viewed the process of reaching this sort of inner harmony in the same way that one would cultivate a garden:

> One can dispose of one's drives like a gardener and, though few know it, cultivate the shoots of anger, pity, curiosity, vanity as productively and profitably as a beautiful fruit tree on a trellis; one can do it with the good or bad taste of a gardener and, as it were, in the French or English or Dutch or Chinese fashion; one can also let nature rule and only attend to a little embellishment and tidying-up here and there; one can, finally, without paying any attention to them at all, let the plants grow up and fight their fight out among themselves indeed, one can take delight in such a wilderness, and desire precisely this delight, though it gives one some trouble, too. All this we are at liberty to do: but how many know we are at liberty to do it? Do the majority not believe in themselves as in complete fully-developed facts? Have the great philosophers not put their seal on this prejudice with the doctrine of the unchangeability of character?

At liberty to do? Yes, Nietzsche was skeptical of free will as we tend to look at it—where one is entirely responsible for one's choices and decisions. But he nonetheless advocated for a sort of liberty towards self-expansion and nurturing our will to power. To do this would require a diligent gardener, of course. One would have to water the plants just enough and provide just enough sunlight. They would have to be moderate in the extent to which they allow one drive to conquer another drive. Is this not where we started off? Aristotle's idea of the good life is one of moderation and the cultivation of virtue.

We have come quite a way from struggling with our existential crisis. We have grappled with identity, freedom, and now desire in the form of the will to power. To piece a few of these disparate philosophies together, we could conclude the following. Firstly, we may not have free will in the way we previously thought. Secondly, the good life is one lived in the pursuit of a sort of happiness that goes beyond mere pleasure and pain. It involves a sort of desire for increasing self-complexity and self-expansion. This can be called the will to power—the desire to unfold one's being through growth and action. A scientifically sound method of doing so can be found in flow activities that offer a sense of increasing self-complexity through challenging oneself.

But how is this achieved? Relying on Aristotle's list of virtues, while a step in the right direction, doesn't necessarily honor Nietzsche's belief that we should cultivate our own values. But how do we cultivate our own values? How do we unify all of these internal drives? How do we—in Nietzschean terms—become who we are?

Chapter 26

The Autotelic Personality

One key piece to the puzzle could be found in curiosity. The philosopher John Dewey suggested that innate curiosity and interest are fundamental ingredients in terms of self-expansion. As he argued, this sort of intrinsic fascination with the world energizes our capacity to follow our inherent growth tendencies. Look at a child, for example, who simply follows what they find to be inherently interesting or novel. A butterfly. A macaroni noodle on the floor. Clouds. Much of a child's daily routine is spent exploring and integrating that which is outside of themselves into their being (and yes, sometimes this means they will "incorporate" it by eating it). This curiosity is absolutely necessary as fuel for growth and self-expansion. However, Dewey argues that as we grow older, we often lose this incessant desire to play and explore. We come to form entrenched views of the world and who we are. This is reflected in the sort of overidentification we may experience depending on which social roles we endorse as truly and fundamentally who we are. Yes, in limiting our curiosity, we do gain some sense of security and stability. Sure, we fulfill the need for unity and coherence. However, what we fundamentally lose out on is growth. Specifically, we lose out on the seemingly limitless benefits of exploration that come about through an earnest sense of curiosity. He writes:

> The curious mind is constantly alert and exploring, seeking material for thought, as a vigorous and healthy body is on the qui vive for nutriment. Eagerness for experience, for new and varied contacts, is

found where wonder is found. Such curiosity is the only sure guarantee of the acquisition of the primary facts upon which inference must base itself.

How, then, are we to cultivate this sort of curiosity while still maintaining a sense of wholeness? Psychologist James Marcia conceptualizes identity formation as a process that involves exploring and commitment. We spend our lives drifting between states of exploring different identities and values, eventually committing to some, letting go of others, and, finally, settling on some sort of identity. Marcia notes that the first stage, characterized by exploring, is also plagued by an inherent anxiety. The individual does not know who they are. But they are figuring things out. This is likely a familiar feeling for those who have gone through an existential crisis. It can feel like one is floating in the middle of the ocean, moved by nothing more than a desperate urgency to grab hold of anything at all. On one hand, there is a sense of excitement. You are traversing uncharted territories and embarking on a personal journey of self-discovery. But the constant uncertainty can also leave one in a state of unbearable dread. It might feel like you are drowning. Eventually, you might get that urge to commit to something.

And so, the second stage, commitment, minimizes anxiety through an active commitment to certain goals and roles. Whether it's a job, a relationship, a trip around the world, or simply the development of a morning routine, the stage of commitment should greet us, we hope, after a long period of deliberate and anxiety-ridden uncertainty. However, it should be highlighted that committing to things is often easier said than done. In a world of endless opportunity, one might still feel like there is something more out there—that they have been tied down by a relationship or career that is wrong for them. When committing to things, we might feel like we are compromising ourselves in some way. Or perhaps we may feel like we are settling. And blindly committing to things to quell our anxiety might not be the best idea.

Instead of being anxious, we could end up depressed—a prisoner of our own poor decision-making. What, according to Marcia, is the answer? How do we reap the benefits of exploring while feeling like we are still on stable ground? Marcia argues that we must delicately traverse committing and exploring without either compromising our authentic selves or losing ourselves in an anxious frenzy of non-being. The journey of identity-making must be undertaken with the assumption that we are just as much found as we are created. And so Marcia sees the final identity status, one in which we simultaneously commit to certain social roles while also following our curiosity and exploring, as the most beneficial.

Sure, we may be in a job or have a relationship, but that has not limited us or constrained us to a specific way of life. We avoid Marcelian crispation—that thick ontological crust of overidentification. This balance is reminiscent of our previous discussion on genuine pretending—the capacity to easily adapt to different social roles without becoming too attached to one or another. We can wholeheartedly love our partner, fully commit to our job, or steadfastly support a social cause. But genuine pretending gives us the flexibility to move on when things go awry. A breakup, a layoff, or political disillusionment will not leave us entirely broken. In a sense, balancing the two modes of exploring and committing involves always holding the clarity that change is a constant and that impermanence is the rule rather than the exception. In adopting this sort of identity status, we leave ourselves more capable of adapting and changing while still keeping our feet on the ground—ever ready to experience the meaningfulness that emerges from commitment and sacrifice.

The sort of personality that grows and unifies—explores and commits—reflects the identity that Csikszentmihalyi views as fundamentally conducive to flow activities. This is what Csikszentmihalyi meant by the *autotelic personality*. To be *telic*, in short, is to do something for a goal—with *telos* meaning "goal" in Greek. To be autotelic, then, is to do something for its own sake. The goal is not to do something else—to make money, achieve fame, or reach some other sort of contingent aim. Rather, to be autotelic is to do something because it is intrinsically fulfilling. Recall that flow emerges from a challenge slightly above the skill level needed. The autotelic personality actively seeks out opportunities that can challenge them (of course without overwhelming them).

Does this mean we should pick any challenge? Let us remember, from the very beginning, the nature of our predicament—one that we should never lose sight of. As Heidegger argued, you have been thrown into existence as something—or someone—that is specifically *you*. Not your friend. Not your dog. Not the president. But you—with your own unique proclivities, idiosyncrasies, and preferences! This is where a lot of self-help guides fall short in terms of advising one to do this or that. There needs to be a steadfast recognition that, at the end of the day, only you know what is true to you. Namely, there are certain activities and behaviors that, if followed through with, will make you feel like *you* are becoming yourself. You can take some actions that are better than others, at least in terms of your own process of organismic integration. This prioritization of following one's heart is one of the central themes running along the work of Herman Hesse. Hesse, a life-long appreciator of Nietzschean individualism, would always situate his protagonists in a dilemma of personal struggle between values and desires. What is the right way? Is there a right way? Nowhere is this more apparent than in his novel *Siddhartha*. Hesse wrote:

> Like a veil, like a thin mist, a weariness settled on Siddhartha, slowly, every day a little thicker, every months little darker, every year a little heavier…He only noticed that the bright and clear inward voice, that once awakened in him and had always guided him in his finest hours, had become silent.

This passage comes from the chapter titled "Samsara." Our protagonist has spent the majority of the book in pursuit of enlightenment. He had studied scriptures, lived brutally as an ascetic, and had even met the Buddha. In each instance, Siddhartha was guided by an inner voice urging him to follow his own path. Even in his encounter with the Buddha, and in spite of his praise for his teachings, Siddhartha turns away.

> But there is one thing that this clear worthy instruction does not contain; it does not contain the secret of what the Illustrious One himself experienced—he alone among hundreds of thousands… That is why I am going on my way—not to seek another and better doctrine, for I know there is none, but to leave all doctrines and all teachers and to reach my goal alone or die.

But now Siddhartha has lost this voice. Why?

> The world had caught him; pleasure, covetousness, idleness, and finally also that vice that he had always despised and scorned as the most foolish—acquisitiveness.

Siddhartha eventually becomes a wealthy entrepreneur with a beautiful lover and a great deal of possessions. He is, by all accounts, materially satisfied. And he has even begun to see the wisdom in Samsara, in the ups and downs of the dance itself. Kids, marriage, property. They certainly brought him feelings of fulfillment and purpose. But the silencing of his voice troubled him. In his pursuit of nirvana, he had lost himself somewhere along the way.

Part 4

Being Yourself

In this final part, we will look at how we can go about following our hearts. What are our own drives? Where do they lead us? What does it mean to love something and someone? What is desire? And how can we lead a life that is truly worth living for us personally?

Who could have predicted that the solution to your existential crisis is *being true to yourself*? How obvious! This is perhaps the most cliché resolution to any narrative—a sentimental prayer. However, when discussing being true to oneself, we immediately involve some of the most complex philosophical questions concerning self-knowledge, freedom, and desire. What does it mean to be true to you? Is such a process even possible?

We come out of our inquiry from the previous chapter with a few possible answers. For one, being true to oneself is somewhat measurable. It means that one is experiencing autonomy—a sense of volition—and that this experience results in increased self-complexity. It means some sort of self-expansion or unfolding of being—an implicit sense that one is becoming even *more* than they were before through challenging themselves and stretching their capabilities. These are flow activities—those experiences in which we lose ourselves in the task at hand.

Perhaps we have little in the way of freely choosing which activities or experiences will lead to this sort of self-determination. For some, it may be in knitting. And for others, it may be through singing and dancing. Where does this leave us with freedom? In some sense, the matter of whether we have free will or not is a question that far exceeds the scope of this book. The language of freedom and agency is so embedded in how we refer to our relationship with the world that it would be tricky to imagine a life led by an absolute recognition that everything is predetermined. The question of how one should live if there is no free will already reflects an inherent irony to the situation at hand. To ask this is to presume that we have some say in choosing how we live. According to hard determinists, we have no say in how we would live in the absence of freedom. The question is, by all accounts, absurd.

Harry Frankfurt directly confronts the challenge of living without free will in his ideas of first- and second-order desires. First-order desires are all of those wishes and wants that we find ourselves driven towards simply because we want them. We want to have sex. We want to pet a dog. We want to learn how to skateboard. They are aspirations that are intrinsic in motivation and guided by little conscious reason or justification. In contrast, second-order desires are those we desire to desire (to eat healthy, for example). We may desire to eat ice cream, which is a first-order desire. But this comes into contact with our second-order desire to eat healthy. Frankfurt argues that if there is any freedom of choice, it is in the alignment between these first- and second-order desires. We may have little say in what we desire. But with a determined process of self-insight and self-discovery, we could, at the very least, understand ourselves better to move towards this sort of alignment. In terms of flow activities, these are activities that reflect such an alignment. They are things that we do for ourselves and fulfill our more second-order desires. Under Frankfurt's idea of alignment, we could aspire to organize our lives in such a way that we could engage more frequently in these activities. We could cultivate an autotelic personality and live fully in a state of flow. Ideally, we could cultivate that Nietzschean garden that allows for the unity of our drives. So now we must ask ourselves: *How do we follow our desires in accordance with this aim of self-determination?* More plainly put, we may ask ourselves: *How do we follow our hearts?* To answer this question, we must first turn to the pernicious concept of desire.

Chapter 27

Desire

Nietzsche's will to power has sometimes been taken to represent what we may call desire, defined by Deleuze as "the fundamental principle of ontology, that which underlies the world itself and all of existence and which operates through us as human beings."

Desire is the underlying fuel of our existence. And so the absence of desire is a cessation of life itself. This is perhaps why depression, characterized by a total lack of interest, enjoyment, or pleasure in life, is so closely aligned with thoughts of suicide. Depression can be seen as a fundamental lack of desire—the plateauing of the sort of desire and energy that would otherwise push us towards growth and self-complexity. Desire is a life force that, yes, complexifies life, but it also makes our existence entirely worth living. Without it, we become passionless husks of flesh and bone—aimless wanderers who live to survive rather than thrive. It is only in the execution of our desires (emphasis on *our*) that we find such holistic satisfaction.

And it is uncertain as to whether we have control over our desires. Why are we compelled towards one hobby or one person over another? Recall the intrinsic inclinations that Julia Serano proposes when discussing the importance of gender. Through some mix of factors, biological and social, some of us are pulled towards one gender expression while others of us are pulled towards another. We may desire to express ourselves in one way or another. On a broader scale, beyond a discussion of gender, one could argue that our desires inform our sense of identity. Our intrinsic inclinations, proclivities, and curiosities pull us towards various interests that make up who we are and who we might become.

Therefore, the freedom and agency we strive for to pursue these desires become crucial to our very being. If restricted, we find ourselves unable to become who we are. In other words, our ability to chase and satisfy our desires could be seen as autonomy in action. It characterizes our ability to be free—to execute our will. Regarding our discussion of the two types of freedom, negative liberty gives us the space to pursue these desires. And positive liberty is the fulfillment of these desires. We may have an ambiguous desire to simply express ourselves as we wish. Our parents, teachers, or peers may limit us in some way. Our first task, then, is to free ourselves from the constraints of others. But this does not solve the problem of how exactly we express ourselves. What do we desire when left unencumbered and unconstrained? Positive liberty is the freedom to act on and attain specific desires—the desire to become who you wish to be.

In other words, who you wish to become is the will to power that Nietzsche had in mind when he discussed the innate and organismic self-expansion that fuels our behavior. However, Nietzsche was far from clear and concise in offering us an unambiguous definition of what this could look like. The task of further elaborating on the will to power as a psychological principle was, fortunately, taken up by Deleuze, who equated it fundamentally with the notion of desire. Deleuze (and his cowriter Félix Guattari) were primarily interested in understanding why we sometimes desire our own repression. Why do people vote for dictators, stay in abusive relationships, and join cults? Whereas Fromm looked at the burden of freedom as the answer to this question, Deleuze sought the answer in desire. But to understand his argument, we must first understand what he meant by desire.

Both the will to power and desire can be seen as unconscious and impersonal forces that constantly flow to and fro within the organism—in a blind struggle to continuously grow and expand. But Deleuze takes it a step further: Desire is not just a flowing current—it is a machine. It is simultaneously producing and produced. It is a unit of striving and expansion but without any closed identity—an open and porous system of continual struggle. Perhaps we can describe it as a machine—"an ongoing process of becoming that is the becoming of reality." It is a machine that is fundamentally trying to change, expand, grow, and become something else. Sounds familiar? Recall Camus's idea that the human individual is a creature that is always refusing to be what it is. Perhaps, from this, we can take humanity as the greatest unit of this sort of desiring-production—an organism that is conscious enough to fulfill this constant process of self-overcoming through autonomous decision-making.

Desire, then, is a machine that produces more desire. It is not leading to anything in particular beyond its own growth and expansion. This explains, for example, why we may feel conflicted in terms of which choice is most representative of who we are. Do I go to grad school? Do I break up with my partner? We try our best to dig deep into ourselves, but we can often find that such a process leaves us more confused than before. That is because these drives—these desires—do not necessarily represent varying levels of who we authentically are on the inside. Rather, they represent varying levels of self-expansion. Instead of asking who we are, Deleuze's notion of desire asks us to ponder over who we could be. Which choice will lead to greater self-complexity and novelty?

For Deleuze, we are simply an ongoing collection of competing desires that are always striving and becoming (much like Nietzsche's competing drives[†]). There is no I in the sense that this I is composed of nothing more than an ever-changing flow of desire (or, as Deleuze calls them, "little witnesses") that form our experience of subjectivity. For Deleuze, this feeling of being a subject is little more than an illusion of

---

† Perhaps this reminds you of the concept of the hedonic treadmill—that we return to a baseline of happiness after a positive event occurs, suggesting that an eternal or persistent state of happiness is either impossible or extremely rare for most of us.

time. "The subject, at root, is the synthesis of time." We are time itself. How we experience ourselves, then, is through the continual struggle and synthesis of desires through time. Becoming, then, can be seen as a fairly unconscious process—one that involves the unfolding of these desires at all times.

This is illustrated brilliantly when Siddhartha, after decades of soul-searching, has reserved himself to the life of a ferryman. Sitting at the edge of the river one day, he finally sees the secrets of enlightenment. "He saw that the water continually flowed and yet it was always there; it was always the same and yet every moment it was new." Siddhartha realized that life, too, is an endless process of moving towards something, and yet this constant motion sustains life itself. His sense of self was simply the unfolding of his journey—a journey sustained and catalyzed by a restless and curious seeking. And what sustains this motion? Desire—the inner drives that constantly unfold, expand, and *become*. Siddhartha understood that to frame his life as seeking something specific was damaging. He was seeking the perfect thing to settle on that would give him enlightenment. In doing so, he felt like a failure, unable to solve his existence. But it was only when he realized that life is a mystery—a process of endless bewilderment and disorientation, and that his whole being is composed of all of these experiences and failures and lost loves and new friends—that he found enlightenment.

This is a crucial insight. It is not as if Siddhartha found some sort of inner voice that represents who he is at his very core. Rather, he recognized his subjectivity as dynamic—as a process. Who we are is sustained by growth, motion, and the unfolding of being that is becoming. Our self is a process that gives us the appearance of something stable and static. All of those mistakes, accidents, and seemingly wrong turns are all we are—the continual movement of subjectivity fueled by a synthesis of time and desire. To follow our heart is to embrace this flowing current—*to go with the flow.* Who we are, then, becomes a matter of perdurance—a persistent sense of linking desires through time that flows forward like a river. And so, rather than Descartes's idea of us as thinking beings, we find ourselves, instead, as temporal beings. Our being is marked by time. And this is sustained through desire.

Chapter 28

Alienation

Unfortunately, when we look at modernity, everything is backward. Instead of being defined by time, we use time to serve our own purposes. We see time as separate. We instrumentalize it—and, in doing so, we instrumentalize ourselves. Does this make any sense at all? We are in a constant frenzy—trying to figure out who we are and maximizing the little time we have to become who we are as quickly as possible. Recall our discussion of self-exploitation—of the entrepreneur who simply cannot waste any time. They can't just go with the flow! They can't follow their desires, let alone their curiosity. Everything is now instrumentalized. And so the skills needed to follow our hearts have been forgotten. You can't just sit by a river and deliberate over your sense of identity! Much of what compels us into this sense of allo-exploitation and the resulting alienation can be pinned on the speed of modernity. Hartmut Rosa notes that speed is at the heart of modernization. "Acceleration is a totalitarian force where pressure is felt at all levels."

According to Rosa, the pressure of speed is a constant strain on everyone. For some, the pressure of time comes from the internal drive to constantly upgrade and improve oneself. The materially well-off, for example, fear wasting their time and will compel themselves to exercise, socialize, and maximize their capital lest they lose their fleeting mortal hours. This is the pressure of time that emerges from within—from an inner sense that one must be always improving, always doing *more*. However, time pressure can also be imposed on us from the outside. Our boss or manager has given us a deadline, and it must be obeyed, or we risk financial ruin. And for some, such as the unemployed, time pressure can be experienced as a tremendous sense of lagging behind. Society still ostracizes them, for they have failed to subject themselves to the dominance of speed and efficiency. They lack an identity due to the absence of time pressure. Regardless of where one is in modern society, the result of this pressure at all levels is a guaranteed instrumental relation to the world, where friends become competition and lunch breaks become moments for self-improvement. The constant processing of information has led to a feeling of inner chaos. Where do we go? What are we to do? And how do we survive? There is an existential stiffness. We no longer feel that we are ourselves. This, according to Rosa and many other theorists, is the cause of alienation.

So, what is this alienation? Simply put, when we experience alienation, we do not feel at *home* with ourselves, with others, and with the world around us. Home, I would argue, is a place (or rather a feeling) that allows us to act freely as ourselves. It is a sense of familiarity and connection with the world around us. We are disconnected and struggle in solitude with a "*relationship of non-relationship.*" In other words, we find ourselves beside others in the same spaces, such as the bus or supermarket. But we are not together with them. We are fundamentally isolated from connection and a sense of camaraderie with ourselves and those around us. If we wish to be truly free, capable, and creative creatures, then the issue of overcoming alienation should be considered more seriously. Namely, we must ask ourselves: *Is there a way out of this alienation?*

Resonance

Hartmut Rosa asks an important question: "What would a non-alienated way of life look like?" His answer is found in his idea of *resonance*. Resonance is a specific relationship between you (the subject) and the world (the object) that is reciprocal and leads to mutual transformation. It is experienced in the feeling of answering a call in some sense. We carry out our lives, then, in anticipation of such a call—leaving ourselves open to be influenced and affected by the world around us and willing to change and adapt as necessary. Going beyond mere ideas of the good life that can appear as simple bucket lists of what exactly you want to do, resonance permits destabilization and dynamic playfulness that leave any sort of predictability out of it. We actively seek out things that resonate with us. Sound familiar? The resonant personality and the autotelic personality are perhaps one and the same. They are each actively fueled by a sense of intrinsic curiosity that allows for some level of existential destabilization. This is living through desire *or*, in other words, following your heart. As Rosa explains:

> (Resonance is) a kind of relationship to the world, formed through affect and emotion, intrinsic interest, and perceived self-efficacy, in which subject and world are mutually affected and transformed. Resonance is not an echo but a responsive relationship, requiring that both sides speak with their own voice. This is only possible where strong evaluations are affected. Resonance implies an aspect of constitutive inaccessibility. Resonant relationships require that both subject and world be sufficiently "closed" or self-consistent so as to each speak in their own voice, while also remaining open enough to be affected or reached by each other. Resonance is not an emotional state, but a mode of relation that is neutral with respect to emotional content.

To be resonant is not to be entirely without any notion of subjectivity or self. There is still a personality. But it is a subjectivity driven by intrinsic motivation and curiosity—with a focus on temporarily losing oneself to the world at large if only to return as something more. The resonant subject is one that is in love with life itself.

Chapter 29

Love

Could one experience love under alienation? Alienation, after all, is a state of isolation and existential stiffness. It does not allow for the sort of openness to influence that resonance requires. And this is perhaps why it is easier to remain in a state of alienation. To be affected by something or someone is terrifying. Deleuze even likens it to madness. Is it not? We risk destabilizing ourselves and becoming something else. But this existential project of self-expansion and growth is one that inevitably entails this risk. We must venture outwards if we wish to follow these inner potentialities. And love may be the greatest act of such irrationality. We commit ourselves to something or someone that will inevitably fail us—through death, heartbreak, or some other unpredictable outcome. Nonetheless, we surmount our fears of vulnerability and entrust in ourselves that this incorporation of the Other is still entirely worth the risk. Yes, it may verge on self-destructive at times. And yet the unfolding of love often sustains life itself. For many thinkers, such as Albert Camus, love is the very force that justifies life and its inherent suffering. He writes: "The misery and greatness of this world: it offers no truths, but only objects for love. Absurdity is king, but love saves us from it."

Now, what is love exactly? Yes, of course, there is romantic love—the sort that involves erotic fixation, infatuation, and that feeling of completeness when we are with our beloved. But thinkers such as Simone de Beauvoir have noted that this sort of obsessiveness fails to truly reflect the profundity of *true love*. Such codependence and severe attachment could minimize the transformational aspects of love that are relevant to our journey towards heightened self-complexity. Beauvoir saw most relationships falling into the category of narcissism and devotion—with each partner using the other for their own existential satiation. The narcissist seeks partners that will shower them with love and affection—with a sustained sense of self-importance. The devoted will find a partner they can admire fervently, expecting to be accepted into their beloved's special world. In both cases, each partner will inevitably come to resent the other.

The narcissist will lose respect for their partner. And the devotional lover will come to see their seemingly perfect partner as a human being with flaws, leading to an eventual disillusionment. Each dynamic fails to treat the Other fully as a human subject—as someone with their own desires and drives.

Beauvoir advocated for something that she called *authentic love*—a love that respects the autonomy of their partner because they love them for who they are. Our beloved is treated above all as an unencumbered and unconstrained subject, as another human that is to be truly loved and desired for who they are and who they could become. For Beauvoir, this authentic love allows each partner to reap the benefits of a relationship more broadly, with the benefits being the ability to expand and grow *with* and *through* one another.

The feminist writer bell hooks likewise offered a relevant definition of this sort of authentic love: the will to extend oneself for the purpose of nurturance for both oneself and the other. hooks considered love to be rooted in both intention and action. We do not merely experience it as a passive participant when we are in love. We also demonstrate our love through acts and behaviors. Through this, we grow, and so too does the object of our affection. In some sense, hooks's and Beauvoir's notions of love capture the self-complexity and expansion we have previously discussed. Love is the becoming of oneself through another, all while they do the same. For hooks, this is the main driver of life and identity. She writes:

If I were really asked to define myself, I wouldn't start with race; I wouldn't start with blackness; I wouldn't start with gender; I wouldn't start with feminism. I would start with stripping down to what fundamentally informs my life, which is that I'm a seeker on the path…a path about love.

In some sense, hooks is offering a different concept of the will from that of Nietzsche or Schopenhauer. hooks present us, instead, with another theory of human motivation that is distinct and yet consistent with what we have discussed before. It is a *will to love*—the fundamental impulse towards incorporation and reciprocation with the Other—that informs life. Perhaps this is all we are truly driven by—the need to integrate with that which we are not. Love is desire at its most profound, as it allows us to be in a constant process of both being and becoming. We change slightly in the gaze of the Other, and we hope they do, too, as a result of being exposed to who we are on a deeply intimate level. This is perhaps why Deleuze considered love to be a form of madness. Falling in love necessitates a fundamental shift in perspective—an alteration in how one sees the world and oneself. The lovers initiate a process of collective insanity. And through this dynamic, no matter how long or short it may be, something new and unpredictable is created in the merging of the multiplicities that compose the inner worlds of each participant.

We should not underplay the fact that this encounter with the Other will always involve a great risk. We must give ourselves a little. We must show our cards and open up in ways that we might find distressing. And this process is to be undertaken with an understanding that there are no guarantees, and that this may all be for naught. And yet this act of sacrifice in the face of uncertainty only underscores the power of our will to love. Yes, there are painful risks. Heartbreak. The loss of our beloved. The tragedy of growing apart. At the same time, opening oneself up to love seems entirely worthwhile, even in the face of potential self-destruction and chaos. We engage in one of the most fruitful arenas of self-complexity—in which we engage with the world through the Other as they do the same with us. Late-night conversations in bed. Sharing your favorite songs. A walk in the park. Seemingly mundane rituals of daily existence are now illuminated by their presence. If loved in just the right way, we may even begin to feel like we can be ourselves around them. And, with time, we may even feel more like ourselves than before.

What are these risks that we sign ourselves up for when faced with the prospect of romantic love? Love with another always risks toxicity, heartbreak, and disappointment. A breakup may be characterized by a sense of total loss as one's identity was, at one time, so intimately wrapped up in the identity of one's partner. A future may not appear worth living for as all future plans involve the former partner. The return to the dating scene as a fresh single can be a miserable experience as we subject ourselves to a mundane conversation over drinks—all in the hopes of resecuring that long-lost flame in a blind date or Tinder match. Modern love is often riddled with disappointment. The sociologist Eva Illouz has described the sort of trials and tribulations inherent in the modern dating scene with horrid precision:

> In fact, few people living in the contemporary era have been spared the agonies of intimate relationships. These agonies come in many shapes: kissing too many frogs on the way to Prince/ss Charming; engaging in Sisyphean Internet searches; coming back lonely from bars, parties, or blind dates. When relationships do get formed, agonies do not fade away, as one may feel bored, anxious, or angry in them; have painful arguments and conflicts; or, finally, go through the confusion, self-doubts, and depression of break-ups or divorces. These are only some of the ways in which the search for love is an agonizingly difficult experience from which few modern men and women have been spared. If the sociologist could hear the voices of

men and women searching for love, s/he would hear a long and loud litany of moans and groans.

Dating apps, hook-up culture, and therapy-speak can easily depersonalize the expected intimacy and vulnerability that we tend to associate with romantic situations. Date after date. Ghosting. The feeling that, yes, there are plenty of fish, but your bait is defective. That will to love may inevitably shrink, and soon, we might even find ourselves panicking at the idea of a first date or flirting with a stranger. Why get your hopes up?

While we may not be able to control how others behave in a romantic dynamic, I do think that love is nonetheless a worthy venture for those who wish to grow and learn about themselves. Specifically, romantic love can teach us the importance of detachment. To love without attachment is, above all else, to get over oneself. In fact, Erich Fromm recognizes the overcoming of one's narcissism as the main condition for the achievement of love. In attempting to secure our own self-image through another, we create an image or fantasy of that other. We imprison them there through manipulation, deception, and control. This is our attempt to possess. And we also imprison ourselves in our own narcissism. We cut ourselves off from being able to experience true love. "To abandon the present in order to look for things in the future is to throw away the substance and hold onto the shadow," writes the Buddhist monk Thich Nhat Hanh.

As Beauvoir previously suggested, in order to truly love someone, we must embrace a sense of detachment. But how could one take on such a difficult task, potentially riddled with rejection and betrayal? Firstly, love involves some level of objectivity. You need to see people for their own potentialities and your own potentialities rather than the images you have of them. This, in itself, means abandoning one's self-prioritization. It involves humility. And this humility is informed by a significant faith that through recognizing, trusting, and nurturing you and your partner's potential, love will flourish. Yes, boundaries still exist in this state. But this comes about through education rather than manipulation.

By telling them your boundaries, you hope this will also teach you about them and their boundaries and needs. And they might not be compatible with yours. And here is the crucial and scary part about love without attachment: You must be vulnerable to what you fear. Those things might not last. People might die, or you both may simply drift apart. Feelings change. All you can do is have some humility and faith that the learning process itself, which is reciprocal, will bring love to both. This is perhaps why the spiritual philosopher Jiddu Krishna-murti argues that passion comes through learning rather than through mere gratification. Love emerges within this intense curiosity we have for the other. And how could we truly know those who we supposedly love if we limit them for our own gratification? We must listen without judgment. We must love without attachment. As bell hooks writes: "True love is unconditional, but to truly flourish it requires an ongoing commitment to constructive struggle and change."

Perhaps you do not necessarily have to rely on a messy Other to pursue this path on the way towards love. What if you could learn to love life itself? One of the most constraining perspectives to hold on to is the idea that love is only ever possible in a romantic context. Yes, the admiration and reciprocity experienced between individuals are certainly powerful. But love can exist in many other ways—between the self, the world, and others. This is resonance, as Rosa proposes. We open ourselves up to the world, understanding that we may be changed as a result and that the world, likewise, may be altered by our presence. To do this is to embrace an autotelic personality—to be in a state of constant curiosity and flow, engaged and fully present with one's environment and those who share our space. This is also Aristotle's eudaimonia, the process of living excellently and, through this, deriving some sense of enjoyment from the act of living itself. We fall in love with life. And through this, we become happy.

Chapter 30

Happiness

The claim that happiness will be waiting for us as we come closer to living in a resonant and autotelic manner is fairly consistent with several of the other arguments we have made throughout this book. The claim here, in simple terms, is that happiness is a byproduct of a meaningful life. Happiness, if you recall, is the outcome of living excellently, according to Aristotle. Eudaemonia is the sort of meaningful happiness that arrives from striving for and achieving certain life goals. Similarly, Nietzsche claimed that the will to power is a recipe for happiness. As he wrote, "What is happiness? The feeling that power is growing, that resistance is overcome." This sort of self-expansion and demonstration of competence, aligned with both eudaemonia and the will to power, could also be associated with the state of *flow*—the psychological experience that emerges when one is engaging in an activity that leads to greater self-complexity.

As a result, those who experience flow often experience a form of enjoyment that is far more lasting and substantial than mere pleasure. In fact, the idea that happiness results from pursuing meaning is evident in psychological literature. Self-determination psychologists Veronika Huta and Richard Ryan have demonstrated that those who set and achieved goals that were considered to be meaningful (attaining a job, joining a gym, writing a novel) experienced far more sustained meaning *and* happiness than individuals who pursued goals that were in the service of solely enhancing happiness (such as trying new food or playing games with friends). Those who pursued goals that aligned with meaning and happiness—that is, those whom researchers considered as having been living a *full life*—also experienced greater vitality. Vitality, in their words, refers to a sense of energy and transcendence.

In my own language, I would consider vitality to be the sort of happiness that emerges from being in love with life itself. The resonant individual or the autotelic personality is someone who expresses a great deal of vitality—a wakefulness and sense of awe with the world around them that is derived from a mindful and enthusiastic engagement with whatever the task is at hand. This is an expression of desire at any moment. And so, perhaps more so than a deactivation of desire, depression could be characterized as an absence of vitality. Without even being depressed, an existential crisis could easily erode this sort of energetic state. It is difficult to feel like your life is *vital* or worth living in a state of ontological uncertainty. You will likely feel hopeless, lost, and entirely confused. How could one act spontaneously and engage with the world around them when all they see is misery and anguish?

Chapter 31

The Absurd

We have come full circle. In our existential crisis, we see an inherent lack of vitality. We cannot love our life, let alone accept it. Life has betrayed us. Who we thought we were and how we thought the world worked has been thrown entirely off course. In such circumstances, how could one possibly fall in love with life? Let us first frame our existence as if it were a relationship that we were in. From birth, we find that we are in a constant dynamic with ourselves—specifically with our sense of self and the universe. Certainly, if we are blessed with a happy enough childhood, this relationship with ourselves and the world is a positive one. But with time, like any long-term relationship, we may find ourselves questioning the point of it all. Why continue the relationship? Why not just break up? This is the core of our existential crisis—a period marked by a serious dialogue over whether existence itself is worth a damn. For those in the midst of such existential befuddlement, they may argue that this relationship is somewhat toxic. We cast out our concerns, our prayers, and our desires to understand and comprehend our place in the world outwards in the hope that somebody or something will answer us. But this is to no avail. Like an indifferent lover, the starry night sky offers little clarity or reassurance. The universe is silent to our existential despair. Our existence is left unanswered.

What, then, are our options? Albert Camus identified this sort of relationship we have with existence as the *Absurd*: the tension between our need for meaning and the silent indifference of the world. Once in confrontation with the Absurd, Camus proposed that we have three ways of handling this existential predicament. For one, we could develop some sort of justification for our relationship with the world. And so many turn to religion or some form of ideology in order to cling to a sense of meaning.

However, this is difficult to do under postmodern conditions, and Camus evidently does not advocate for such a path forward. God is dead. No meta-narratives are left standing for long. Camus considered this route to be a form of philosophical suicide and even argued that the existentialists, such as Sartre and Kierkegaard, were still, in a sense, coping through the idea that they could somehow create their own meaning. Camus was adamant that once we are truly aware of the absurdity of our condition, any attempt to reason our way out of it is simply escapism.

According to Camus, the second option is to "exit" the relationship. To kill oneself. To do so is to announce that one has lost their love for life—that the relationship is simply not worth it in the end. While Camus sees this as illogical, I do think that this is a personal decision at the end of the day. Who is to say how unreasonable it is to end one's life? David Foster Wallace likens it to someone in a burning building, with the least painful option being to avoid the flames and jump out of the window. For many, this *isn't* the best option. But for some of us, we are thrown into a world that is on fire at a far too early age. Chronic illness. War. Abuse. It is difficult to lay claim that one has some sort of ethical responsibility to remain alive.

The Myth of Sisyphus

For those still holding on to some will to live, what is Camus's solution to this exactly? The third option, one that may leave the more pessimistic among us quite dissatisfied, can nonetheless be reserved for those who still wish to love life and continue on this path in spite of all misery and tragedy.

In moments of intense despair, I always found comfort in the closing line of his "Myth of Sisyphus": "One must imagine Sisyphus happy." I've often taken it to mean that regardless of external circumstances, there is some choice in my reaction to things. According to Greek mythology, Sisyphus, the King of Ephyra, was condemned to roll a rock up a hill for eternity as punishment for tricking the gods. His endless toil, a futile act of suffering that he is forced to partake in daily, intensifies each time he watches the boulder roll back down. In his description of the Absurd, Camus saw Sisyphus's situation as analogous to that of modern humanity. We must toil away each day, commuting and working, with no fundamental reason behind it all. For most, the Absurd remains hidden, and so the modern individual goes about their existence with little more than a vague sense of existential restlessness. But Camus is interested in those special few who, in a sudden flash of horrid lucidity, find themselves facing a world "divested of light and illusions." They see who they are and what they are doing as utterly meaningless. They see the Absurd. By all accounts, they experience an existential crisis. And so, the options of escapism (through ideology or hedonism) and escape (through suicide) appear as perfectly acceptable.

But what about Sisyphus? He doesn't fill his days with drugs nor Netflix. Nor does it appear possible for him to simply end his life. By divine command, he is ordered to roll a boulder up a hill eternally after all! Camus likely saw Sisyphus as the perfect candidate in terms of proving whether life was worth living in spite of such irrefutable absurdity. If Sisyphus could find happiness, perhaps so could we. And Camus affirms that such a state is possible: *One must imagine Sisyphus happy.* However, understanding Camus's argument for how such happiness is possible is far from clear. I have often found myself questioning the premise of Camus's argument. If life is truly terrible, if identity is impossible, and if freedom is illusory, isn't this just a big cope? Doesn't this amount to simply telling a depressed or traumatized or helplessly unsure and disillusioned person that they should be happy and smile through the pain? The existential crisis is a condition consisting primarily of intense doubt and skepticism. To accept Camus's affirmation on its own just doesn't cut it. Sisyphus, by all accounts, should be experiencing a tremendous existential crisis. He is condemned for eternity! Why is he happy? Is he stupid?

We should take note of the conditions of Sisyphus and how it relates to our own lives. Sisyphus is in an aversive situation—he is forced to do something that will never work out. His boulder will always roll back down the hill. Similarly, in each of our lives, many, if not all, of our boulders will roll back down the hill. We enter long-term relationships and spend our time pursuing degrees and careers. But ultimately, many of these rocks will descend to the bottom, and after some grief, we will inevitably find new boulders to start rolling back up. Those, too, will be destined to roll back down the mountain. We could even argue that life is really just one big boulder where no matter how much we do, it all will eventually roll back down to its demise.

Learned Helplessness

This hopeless situation, reflected in "The Myth of Sisyphus" and our own predicament, could be explained through the psychological concept of *learned helplessness*. Learned helplessness was first theorized when researchers, upon repeatedly shocking dogs, found that the dogs would eventually give up trying to fight the oncoming shocks. Simply put, they learned to be helpless. Similar research showed that people, when confronted by hopeless situations, will consider themselves to be helpless after they start to realize that nothing they do will change their circumstances. Often, they will come to believe that because nothing worked in this situation, nothing will work in similar situations. They will translate their sense of pessimism and despair to their lives in general. Think of those around you who, after a lifetime of disappointment and failure, resign themselves to lives of quiet cynicism. They view the world as a place that is naturally unjust and themselves as lacking in autonomy. They may develop addictive and self-destructive habits that only further perpetuate their cycle of helplessness. As the years pass, their assumptions prove true. They appear, by all accounts, helpless.

Learned helplessness has also been closely associated with depression—the result of feeling like one is born to suffer for little rhyme or reason. Sisyphus is a prime example of someone subject to such chronic disappointment and potential depression. Psychologists who are privy to such a concept would likely hypothesize that Sisyphus, after realizing time and time again that the rock will roll back down, would likely also learn to be helpless. Based on a past of misery and futility, Sisyphus would, in all likelihood, fail to see a future worth living for. According to psychology, we could adjust Camus's maxim as such: *One should imagine Sisyphus depressed.*

For the rest of us, who are not Kings of Ephyra, learned helplessness manifests in resisting the past through various techniques that, ironically, take away any sense of control we have over our future. Through escapism, we might scroll for hours or drink until the bar closes in order to avoid thinking about our existential condition. Or, we may continually resist accepting what has happened by ruminating over what could have been or what we could have done differently. We may find ourselves lingering on a future that cannot be because it requires us to somehow change the past. This is one of the two demons that drive our existential crisis: the contingency of the past. As long as we fail to accept the permanence of our history, we will be ruled by former events and mishaps. We will find our lives dictated entirely by the past. We will spend our fleeting existence running from the shadow of all that has been done to us.

This is Camus's Absurd in full force. *Why have I been thrown into this identity? Why has my life become a vessel for paying off my student loans? Why did I fall in love with someone who would so abruptly break my heart? And why haven't I recovered yet?* The answers we have for these questions can appear quite practical. We tell ourselves, *"Once I am in a relationship…" "Once I get this job…" "Once I find myself…" "Once*

I get this stupid rock up this stupid hill…" then I'll be happy and find meaning, and all of this suffering will be worth it. We fall for all those false hopes that repeatedly fail to live up to their promise. Through this, we find ourselves entrapped in a state of perpetual disappointment. After failures, breakups, and existential crises, we may simply toss up our hands and declare ourselves helpless in the face of the Absurd.

This isn't a bad place to be. You're further along than most. At least you're aware. But now what? Both Camus and psychotherapy are in agreement with what one should do in such a state of despair: accept it. As the biographer Robert Zaretsky writes: "For Camus, true nobility lies in lucid acceptance of the world, its beauties and its limits, its joys, its demands, its inhabitants and our common lot."

What does this acceptance entail exactly? How could we possibly accept the contingent elements that have left us in such a sorry state? Here, Camus's analogy of a happy Sisyphus is reminiscent of Nietzsche's *amor fati*, the love of one's fate, where we accept ownership of our lives and learn to embrace our existence no matter how imposed it may feel upon us. "My formula for greatness…that one wants nothing to be different, not forward, not backward, not in all eternity…not merely bear what is necessary but love it." Nietzsche imagines a demon visiting him late at night and cursing him with having to experience everything in his life up until that moment for eternity. Would he embrace this curse? For Nietzsche, the individual who has the courage and vitality to accept and embrace what has been done to them will be truly happy. Camus similarly encourages this perspective as he writes: "A will to live without rejecting anything of life, which is the virtue I honor most in this world."

Recall our earlier discussion on identity. We may resent or lament the cards that have been dealt to us in terms of race, physicality, gender, class, or personality. This is the equipment that Alfred Adler spoke of. And it is the contingency of our condition, one of the main drivers of our existential crisis, that can haunt our entire lives. Surely, we may feel a strong urge to change these facts about ourselves in some manner. And certainly, there are some things worth changing if possible. But firstly, we must learn to accept and embrace what has been done to us. This notion of embracing our past is, in a sense, a brave act of love. Here, I see Camus and Nietzsche's philosophy of amor fati as complementary to the will to love.

In the same way that we consider true love to be an act of acceptance of the Other's features and flaws with no expectation to change, I believe that this love of fate is simply authentic love turned inwards. We do not need to give up on who we are. We can still make an effort to change our present situation, especially if it is in our control. Sisyphus, if he could escape from his eternal punishment, should by all means do so. But first, he, like us, must accept what has been done to him. His fate has marked him and shaped him into who he is uniquely. In embracing who we presently are, we follow Adler's advice that what makes someone isn't what has happened to them. Rather, it is what they choose to do with what has happened to them. Our identity is defined, essentially, by what use we make of our equipment rather than the equipment itself.

Acceptance and Commitment Therapy

Confusing? Camus's Sisyphean argument can be further clarified through contemporary psychology. Recall that Sisyphus, by all accounts, is susceptible to learned helplessness. As argued, it is only through an initial acceptance and embrace of his predicament that Sisyphus can free himself. This acceptance of one's current situation and what has happened in the past maps quite nicely onto an empirically valid method in dealing with learned helplessness: acceptance and commitment therapy (ACT).

ACT developed out of recognizing that what people in terrible situations are learning isn't helplessness. Instead, they are forgetting that they have control over their lives. Recall that one of the fundamental drivers of learned helplessness is the sense that one's current situation will translate to future situations. The shocked dog will stop fighting because it comes to expect that another electrocution will always come, regardless of what it decides to do. Similarly, an individual who has experienced a few bad relationships will expect that future romantic prospects will similarly disappoint them. This line of thinking is far from irrational. In fact, it makes perfect sense to expect a terrible future from a terrible past. However, the nefarious strength of learned helplessness lies in its ability to make one forget that they do have some say in the present.

Simply put, the future is not yet written, because the present is in our hands. For those in the pits of hell, this is difficult to see. Instead, the perpetuation of aversive situations and the persistence of suffering convinces us that our future will simply be an echo of our past—as something that has already been written. From this, we relinquish our control over future events. We come to believe, with time, that life happens to us rather than through us.

The first step in ACT, then, is to accept one's thoughts and emotions. Rather than resisting or evading negative reactions (*Why did I date that person?* or *Why have I been condemned for eternity to push this rock up a hill?*), we simply observe our thoughts, such as, "I am having the thought of that time when I dated this person." Do you think this is stupid and cheesy, and whatever you are going through is literally the worst thing ever? Great! Accept that thought with open arms and give it a cup of tea. In doing this sort of radical acceptance, we develop a different sense of self: the *self-as-context*. This self is the observer witnessing our memories, thoughts, and feelings. This is in contrast to seeing oneself in terms of specific attributes, possessions, or social roles, which often involves an overidentification of one's role.

Camus's diagnosis of the Absurd is actually closely tied to this sense of the self as an inexplicable process—the self-as-context—rather than a graspable entity. As he writes:

If I try to grasp this self of which I am assured, if I try to define it and to sum it up, it is no more than a liquid that flows between my fingers. I can depict one by one all the faces that it can assume...this same heart which is mine will ever remain for me undefinable... always shall I be a stranger to myself.

We suffer because we have identified fully with something that has no real self. We care more about what we are rather than what we do. What if we don't need to know who we are in order to be happy? What if we accepted that this quest for absolute self-knowledge is an inherently impossible task, like rolling a rock up a hill that will always fall back down? Let's first and foremost accept that we will never fully know who we are, okay?

Commitment

But what might this look like? Our absurd hero, Sisyphus, shares similarities to the aforementioned Taoist principle of genuine pretending, in which one holds the ability to enact social roles without being tricked into submitting to them or being fully defined by them. The genuine pretender is like a child in play, where they play out different roles while recognizing that such roles hold no inherent value. Think about your childhood and how little you knew yourself. Wasn't that actually kind of freeing? Children embrace transformation, change with ease, and engage in the free wandering of the heart, knowing that their identity is both genuine in what they choose to do and pretend in terms of how much it matters at the end of the day.

However, one issue with embracing this sense of self as a genuine pretender is also taken up in our discussion of freedom. In negative freedom, we have the space to move unconstrained—to be who we wish to be. But this absence of constraints does not point us towards who we would wish to be. Many of our options may appear arbitrary. We still lack clarity over our positive liberty—what we should do with our freedom. Hinted at with the idea of genuine pretending, our acceptance still entails an act of deciding what we should do once we have accepted things.

Acceptance does not need to lead to apathy. Remember, we are accepting things in order to reclaim agency over our lives! And so the next step in ACT is to choose a valued direction. ACT assumes that most of us want to have control over our lives. The main idea is that our resistance to what has happened, or what is happening, has left us out of control of our own lives. Once we have accepted what has happened to us and what we really are, without rigidness or fixation, we can better decide what we want things to be on our own terms, moving forward. We can more clearly see what we value.

A beautiful example of this comes from Csikszentmihalyi's description of an assembly line worker named Rico, whom he interviewed. While most workers were bored and apathetic, resisting a job that was arguably monotonous and undesirable, Rico challenged himself to do his job as perfectly and efficiently as possible. Rico learned to love the exhilaration of using his skills fully. He embraced his present situation. In other words, he had accepted where he was and made the most of it. Rather than use his attention and energy to complain and resist his situation, he embraced his fate and, ironically, changed his situation as a result. His efficiency at his job allowed him to attend college courses at night, greatly opening up his job prospects beyond assembly line work. What is important to note here is that Rico claimed agency over his attitude by first accepting his condition. He then asked himself, plainly, "What can I do next?"

Evidently, Rico exhibits the qualities of Csikszentmihalyi's "autotelic personality." They are doing things for their own sake rather than to achieve some later goal. They experience flow often, the subjective experience of engaging in high-skill and high-challenge activities that result in a loss of a sense of self, enjoyment, and greater life satisfaction. Csikszentmihalyi writes:

Their psychic energy seems inexhaustible. Even though they have no greater attentional capacity than anyone else, they pay more attention to what happens around them, they notice more, and they are willing to invest more attention in things for their own sake without expecting an immediate return.

The autotelic personality, evident in the above quote, is a state of being that requires a fervent and strong-willed sense of commitment. This type of commitment is important, especially for those who undertake acceptance and commitment therapy. Commitment allows us to commit our attention effectively. We don't need to develop a perfect goal or have absolute freedom over our lives to know our next move. But we do need something to orient ourselves towards. This commitment is likewise framed as an integral aspect of harnessing the power of flow, as Csikszentmihalyi notes:

A mountain climber sets her goal to reach the summit not because she has some deep desire to reach it, but because the goal makes the experience of climbing possible. If it were not for the summit, the climb would become pointless ambling that leaves one restless and apathetic.

Commitment Through Acceptance

What is the next action? To make some coffee? To take a walk? To cure cancer? Accomplishing any of these tasks will not complete us or make us eternally happy, but that is simply because there is nothing to complete. We simply are, and will continue to be, until our time is up. What will you do with this time? Accepting rather than resisting our limitations, failures, and mortality is to free one's attentional resources up and become more mindful. By accepting our past, we conserve the energy and vitality that is necessary for committing towards a future that is, in fact, in our control. To do this requires a steadfast and disciplined attempt at mindfulness. And there is admittedly something very Buddhist about the final lines in "The Myth of Sisyphus," in which Sisyphus is fully present and almost lost in the activity of pushing the boulder up the hill. He is, by all accounts, experiencing flow. And in accepting his condition, Camus imagines Sisyphus surmounting any possible despair. Sisyphus has broken the shackles of helplessness and has taken control of his life. He can now decide that, yes, the absurd holds no promises or certainties, but it also still offers objects for love. We, too, can embrace this sort of recognition and love for the here and now. Nature, art, and other living beings. The endless mystery of who we are. Upon acceptance of his situation, Sisyphus commits himself to the beauty of life through the arduous task of happiness.

The philosopher Simone Weil, a great influence on Camus, writes:

> Beauty defeats, if only for short moments, the selfish concerns and preoccupations that mostly govern our lives. Filled with wonder, or filled with love, we forget ourselves—a precondition for making room for others...in order to truly see, to open ourselves to beauty and justice, we must suspend our thought, leaving it detached, empty and ready to be penetrated by the object.

Happiness is something achieved through attention and effort, through accepting the certainty of the past and the uncertainty of the future, and, ultimately, through committing fully to the present. Committing to a life we want involves shedding the influence of learned helplessness that deceives us into believing that the past is the future. Through accepting the past, we see that it does not have to be our future. We free our attention to fall in love with life itself. And so we find ourselves eternally in the present. This is perhaps why Ludwig Wittgenstein, often considered to be one of the greatest philosophers of all time, stated that "if we take eternity to mean not infinite temporal duration but timelessness, then eternal life belongs to those who live in the present."

Will to Happiness

Of course, there is little challenge in waxing poetic about the beauties of existence. But what about all of the horrors? What about all of the unjustified suffering? Some may see Camus's conclusion as far too naive and rosy-eyed. The appropriate question for the skeptic is not "Why is Sisyphus happy?" but rather, "Why should Sisyphus be happy?" The same question I direct to myself at times. *Why should I be happy?* The world can appear exceptionally cruel. I have an endless list of regrets and things I don't like about myself. And no matter what I do, I will die. Now, after accepting these unalterable facts about existence, can I still justify happiness?

Camus flips happiness from something that we should try to gain or accomplish into an ethical commitment: We owe it to the good in the world and ourselves to be happy. Happiness is not something that happens to us or something we get. Rather, it is a will towards happiness, "an enormous, ever-present consciousness…the conscious creation of one's happiness regardless of external circumstances." We owe it to ourselves and others to be happy because there is still beauty in the world and in ourselves that, by its mere presence, can justify existence. "Yes, there is beauty and there are the humiliated. Whatever the difficulties the enterprise may present, I would never like to be unfaithful either to one or the other."

Importantly, happiness should not be seen as an embrace of naive positivity—something that we might call toxic positivity. We should not be in the habit of smiling to simply keep up appearances. Camus even criticized the pathological happiness he sees in American culture when he wrote, "In this country where everything is done to prove that life isn't tragic, they feel something is missing." The happiness of Sisyphus takes into account the tragedy of life and nonetheless pushes forth in the service of an unfolding present. We must maintain our focus on the good and the bad in the world if we wish to rebel against all that threatens its beauty—those objects of love.

In a sense, the happiness Sisyphus enjoys is found in the acceptance in which one feels okay regardless of the outcome. It is the simple choice to accept what has happened and commit to what *is* with no stake in what will come. Certainly, we may experience the sort of hedonic happiness that comes from pursuing and committing to things we value dearly. But that happiness should not be the sole justification of our ventures. Rather, our motivation should ideally emerge from a sense of increasing our self-complexity, of unfolding ourselves in tandem with the world around us. The driving force behind this, love, should be enough. To sustain love, we must maintain a blissful and serene disposition—one that we may call serenity.

Camus asks us to accept that there is no hope and, simultaneously, to insist that this does not mean we should despair. Rather, we should recognize our duty towards ourselves and others in committing to happiness. In an essay titled "Between Yes and No," a much younger and less famous Camus sums up his point clearly: "When we are stripped down to a certain point, nothing leads anywhere any more, hope and despair are equally groundless, and the whole of life can be summed up in an image."

Snippets of the present, a laughing face, a rosy-cheeked lover, that moment in a song that never fails to move you, dancing, porch-light talks with friends, painting, kissing, swimming, awkward hellos and bittersweet goodbyes, tears of joy and despair, the dancing of long grass in the autumn wind, a mother's hug, a stranger's smile, the firsts and lasts, the could-have-beens and never-will-bes, dirty dishes, Sunday coffee, figuring out that math problem, a busker's voice, the pink sky at dusk, seeing your loved ones happy. These are enough. We are all creatures of the Absurd, rolling our rocks up that hill. And it only takes a few of us to take up this duty of happiness, to imagine ourselves happy, and to develop the strength necessary to uplift life in the short time we have. What has happened has happened. And what will happen is never guaranteed.

Now, what would you like to do next? Whatever it is, it will be worthy of loving.

Afterword

A decade after my first trip, I was fortunate enough to revisit Europe. The trip was planned with a friend and was meant to celebrate his recent graduation from law school. It was also planned around a period that I could only describe as yet another existential impasse similar to the one I had experienced as a teen. Only now, I was swimming in deeper waters. I had more of a life and an identity than at fifteen. Certain decisions had been made and had become solid facts about my life. I attended McGill and studied psychology. I had been in and out of relationships. I had a successful YouTube channel. In fact, I had recently hit one million subscribers and yet, unexpectedly, felt a gnawing emptiness upon reaching such a high number. I felt trapped. Is this all that I was meant to do? I struggled to see a future where I would be happy solely pursuing a career online. The lack of stability and the commodification of the self are only a few explanations for why such a thought haunted me. And so my mind shifted between various different life paths. In one, I was enrolled in Columbia's philosophy program and building a relationship with someone who had impacted me greatly. In another, I lived in Barcelona, working on a digital visa and enjoying morning runs on the beach while practicing my Spanish. I imagined myself also moving to Vancouver and possibly pursuing a degree in experimental psychology at UBC, where I would be closer to my family, high school friends, and nature. Sometimes, I even imagined embracing the influencer status and moving to LA to increase my social network. What felt right? Those ancient feelings of idiocy, of utter befuddlement as to what I was to do, emerged slowly but surely as my friend and I traversed the French Riviera and the sunny Italian coast.

For whatever reason, before I flew to Europe, I decided to bring along a copy of Nietzsche's *Beyond Good and Evil.* The book is difficult to read at times. His writing style drifts between detailed philosophical arguments and passionate prose. Sometimes, Nietzsche can articulate ideas that will reach into your chest and rip your heart out. At other times, he sounds like a misogynistic loner, hell-bent on proving his genius by ridiculing those around him. Much like my earlier acquaintance with Camus's detached and indifferent Meursault, I found myself equally disturbed by Nietzsche's writing style. I understood little. I was disturbed by much of it. And yet every once in a while, I would come across a passage that seemed to envisage my entire existence. This was only further emphasized by the context of being back in Europe. I was reintroduced to the feeling of being up close and personal with such a rich intellectual and cultural heritage. I stood in the parks where Picasso had once painted. I reflected on my life in the same harbor that Portuguese explorers once departed from. I could feel that vitality that invigorated my quest for self-understanding a decade ago. It was refreshing. And entirely needed.

While reading on a stony beach in Nice, France, I learned that it was, in fact, the exact location where Nietzsche had written *Beyond Good and Evil.* What are the odds?! In fact, Nietzsche would regularly set out on long, solitary hikes up the mountains to the town of Èze. There was even a trail there commemorating his notable pastime: *Le Sentier Nietzsche.* To make things even better, my friend and I had a day to spare with nothing planned. And so we took the train to the foot of the trail. There was something serene about walking the same trails that Nietzsche once had.

I tried my best to imagine how the landscape had danced with his thoughts—how each peak and valley blended with his life of turbulent highs and lows. Nietzsche was, by all accounts, someone who embraced the life of philosophy. He was persistent in his quest to know *why.* And in this pursuit, he famously suffered a life of solitary madness.

When confronted by those feelings of an existential crisis, of feeling trapped by contingency and confused by arbitrariness, Nietzsche embraced the crisis as a natural state of being. And some would say he suffered for it. But as I hiked up the mountain, I began to see why he thought such a life to be worthy. The Mediterranean coast's vibrant greenery and glowing blue instilled a warm feeling of vitality—a passionate love for life. By deconstructing everything, Nietzsche may have found what truly remained in the end.

It was quite comforting to see a small sign along the trail, left by the town of Èze, commemorating Camus's and Nietzsche's admiration for this region as an example of what makes life worth living. The warm sun. Dancing. Bird songs and the pleasant howl of the wind across the rocky cliffside. This was not an escape from the burden of philosophy for these thinkers. In fact, it was the entire reason why they philosophized. To gesture confidently towards a heaven on Earth, an eternity in the present.

The existential crisis is an anguished grappling with your relationship with life. *What is the point?* You ask this again and again. We are thrown into this world with little reason. And we are forced to make something out of what we have been thrown into. These tools that we have been given are faulty. We are poor. We are traumatized. We are mortal. What are we supposed to do? Who are we supposed to become? Life becomes a problem for us to solve. *If only I was liked more! If only I had some more money or a bit more discipline!* We think the resolution is always in a relationship, job, or accomplishment. And we attain these worthy aims only to find ourselves once again asking, *What is the point?* None of it lasts. And so the promise of lasting happiness fades more and more into the idealism of a distant fairy tale. Life is a problem with no clear parameters beyond the fact that it will end.

The worst thing you could do, then, is to believe that any of this matters, that if you play your cards right, you will find that lasting happiness. Forming a rigid sense of self attempts to alter the unalter-able—to avoid the truth that nothing is eternal and all can be questioned. More importantly, overidentifying (with one's goals, traits, accomplishments, past) limits one from all they could truly be. You may not be able to become who you would like to be. But I would suggest that you still don't know all that you could become. The only way to know this, of course, is to open oneself up to the capricious nature of things. To start where your curiosity leads you. This delicate dance with life may invigorate you. You may encounter aspects of yourself and the world that were once hidden under the frigid shade of your pride. Embrace this! Embarrass yourself. Wheeze and cough on the hiking trail. Trip and fall. And then get up. Again and again. Set your sights on targets offering only the most scenic routes. And fail again and again. This is the most radical path you can take—to passionately pursue something for its own sake. To climb the mountain for the climb and not for the peak.

You will come to learn that this does all, in fact, matter quite a bit. Love and happiness alone justify the horridness and emptiness we may experience with life. There is lightness and beauty everywhere, but only if you are looking hard enough. The only way to do so is, iron-ically, to act as if none of this matters. Embrace roles genuinely, but know that it is all a game of pretend. Work towards goals earnestly, but know that they are excuses for living well and not a reason for living itself. Life, instead, is sustained by small acts of kindness, of open-ness, of understanding. These cannot be planned for. These cannot be scheduled in between meetings or after work. They simply are the things that happen while we are planning. While we are trying to live.

My friend and I reached the top of the trail that flowed into the mountain town of Èze. There was a short passage on another of the signs left on the trail. It was something I had read earlier in the day, the concluding ode to Nietzsche's *Beyond Good and Evil.*

O noon of life! O time to celebrate!
O summer garden!
Restless happiness in standing, watching and waiting: —
I await friends, ready day and night
Where are you friends? Come! It's time! It's time!

Nietzsche awaits friends that will never come. He calls them ghosts of friends, once caring companions who can no longer understand or appreciate his journey of wandering and madness. He fears that they may not even recognize him. Nietzsche has committed himself to a life of radical skepticism and transvaluation—forming values that may be entirely at odds with society around him. In other words, he has committed himself to philosophy. It would make sense, then, that he would grow solitary with his increasing eccentricity. Who would wish to converse with someone so out there? So crazy? He solemnly writes: *Only he who changes remains akin to me.*

Once one has experienced an existential crisis, it could be hard to turn back. You may have isolated yourself. You may have entered unwilling participants into dreary conversations on finitude, nihilism, and misanthropy. A fair amount of Nietzsche's writing reflects this sort of profound pessimism that resonates with the existentially anguished. But I think, on a lighter note, his final remarks reflect the life-affirming urge to philosophize. It is the need to be understood—to feel at one with another, bound by our strange condition.

Philosophy came to me at a time when I felt alone and misunderstood. To enter into this great conversation about the essence of life—love, freedom, fate, desire, goodness, and evil. It has given me the tools to expand this conversation, to reach millions who ask similar questions and enter the same dark nights of the soul I once experienced. With time, the right friends revealed themselves to me. And hiking the trail with one of them created a memory I will treasure for a lifetime. But I could not have done that without first having the courage to be an idiot. To open myself up to the world. To ask questions relentlessly. To fail tremendously. I will never have it all figured out. But that would be boring. So, let us ask questions together. Let us philosophize. And let us argue and laugh and sing and dance until the light fades.

This song is over—the sweet cry of longing
Died in my mouth—
A sorcerer did it, the friend at the right time,
The friend of noon—no! do not ask who he is—
At noon was the time one became two ...

Now we celebrate together, certain of victory,
The feast of feasts:
Friend Zarathustra has come, the guest of guests!
Now the world laughs, the dread curtain is rent,
The wedding has come for light and darkness ...

Acknowledgments

It takes a village to make a book, and there's an endless list of individuals I would like to thank for their support, insight, and guidance throughout this process. For brevity, I want to extend my gratitude to the following people, although I would like to make it clear that this list is far from complete.

Firstly, I would like to thank Robert Pantano for his encouragement, advice, and support through the whole process. This book came from a series of seemingly innocuous emails over whether I should write a book. Without Robert's confidence in my writing, as well as his ability to keep me on schedule and focused, this book would not have happened at all. From this, I would also like to thank Michael McConnell, Tiff Frost, and Mohamad Al-Hakim for their editing and copywriting skills. Their insight and advice truly brought this book to a completely other level in terms of quality and clarity.

Secondly, I would like to thank Izaak Thomas for his personal and professional support throughout. Izaak, my brother and the other half of the Sisyphus 55 YouTube channel, worked tirelessly to create the perfect book cover, and I'd say he did an outstanding job. His eye for design and colour, while keeping in mind my numerous requests, was a necessity in finalizing the cover. And the hours we have spent discussing physics, philosophy, psychology, and life in general greatly informed my writing and the direction of this book.

Thirdly, I'd like to thank the many academics, creatives, and writers who have given me the tools to embark on this journey, including Dr. Richard Koestner, Dr. Anne Holding, James Avery, Eamon Dolan, Mr. Dearden, Mrs. Gaudio, Alex O'Connor, Olivia Sun, F.D. Signifier,

Macken Murphy, Dr. Rachel O'Neil, Dr. Hans-Georg Moeller, Elliot Sang, Kalen, Jacob Ajayii, and Dr. Gerrit Krueper.

Fourthly, I'd like to thank the more than a million people who decided to hit subscribe, for whatever reason. I'm not the best at responding, but please trust that I do read the comments, and I appreciate your support. Thank you for your enthusiasm, insight, and continued confidence in my rambling attempts to find clarity in existence.

Fifthly, I would like to thank the rest of my friends and family for the late-night conversations, challenging discussions, words of wisdom, and all those moments that make life worth something. Specifically, I would like to thank Ryan Holley, Manan Madhok, Blake Enders, and Gabe Wooten-Soe for our longstanding friendship.

Finally, and most importantly, I would like to thank my mom, Kathie, and my dad, Les, for their love, care, support, and patience.

Oh, and my late leopard gecko, Fred. Thank you, Fred.

Bibliography

Part 1

Agarwal, Naresh Kumar. *Exploring Context in Information Behavior:
Seeker, Situation, Surroundings, and Shared Identities*, Vol. 9, Ed. Gary
Marchionini (San Rafael, CA: Morgan & Claypool Publishers, 2017),
11, Citing Michael J. Inwood, A Heidegger Dictionary (Hoboken, NJ:
Wiley, 1999), [Page 7].

Aldrich, J. H., and M. Freeze. *Political Participation, Polarization, and
Public Opinion*. In Facing the Challenge of Democracy. Https://Doi.
Org/10.23943/Princeton/9780691151106.003.0008.

Baum, A et al. "Socioeconomic Status and Chronic Stress. Does Stress
Account for SES Effects on Health?" *Annals of the New York Academy
of Sciences* Vol. 896 (1999): 131-44. Doi:10.1111/j.1749-6632.1999.
Tb08111.x.

Becker, Ernest. *Escape from Evil*. New York: Free Press, 1975.

Billig, Michael. "Comic Racism and Violence." In *Beyond a Joke: The Limits
of Humor*, 25–44. London: Palgrave Macmillan, 2005. Https://Doi.
Org/10.1057/9780230236776_2.

Blacker, David J. "The Illegitimacy of Student Debt." *Cultural Logic:
Marxist Theory & Practice* 2013 (Whole Number 20): 195–208.

Bourdieu, Pierre. *Outline of a Theory of Practice*. Translated by Richard
Nice. Cambridge: Cambridge University Press, 1977.

Boxell, L., M. Gentzkow, J. Shapiro, and National Bureau of Economic
Research. Cross-Country Trends in Affective Polarization. NBER
Working Paper Series, No. 26669. National Bureau of Economic
Research, 2020. Retrieved April 3, 2022.

Brown, D. "How One Man Convinced 200 Ku Klux Klan Members to
Give Up Their Robes." NPR, August 20, 2017. Https://Www.Npr.
Org/2017/08/20/544861933/How-One-Man-Convinced-200-Ku-
Klux-Klan-Members-to-Give-up-Their-Robes. Retrieved April 3, 2022.

Butler, Judith. *Gender Trouble: Feminism and the Subversion of Identity*. New York: Routledge, 1990.

Dahlstrom, Daniel O. *The Heidegger Dictionary*. Malden, MA: Wiley-Blackwell, 2013.

Damasio, Antonio. *Feeling & Knowing: Making Minds Conscious*. New York: Pantheon Books, 2021.

Damian, Rodica I., Markus Spengler, Andreea Sutu, and Brent W. Roberts. "Sixteen Going on Sixty-Six: A Longitudinal Study of Personality Stability and Change Across 50 Years." *Journal of Personality and Social Psychology* 117, No. 3 (2019): 674–695. Https://Doi.Org/10.1037/Pspp0000166.

De Beauvoir, Simone. *The Second Sex*. Translated by Constance Borde and Sheila Malovany-Chevallier. New York: Vintage Books, 2011. Originally Published as Le Deuxième Sexe (Paris: Gallimard, 1949).

Du Bois, W. E. B. *The Souls of Black Folk*. Chicago: A. C. McClurg & Co., 1903.

Ehrenberg, Alain. Ehrenberg, Alain. *The Weariness of the Self: Diagnosing the History of Depression in the Contemporary Age*. (Reprint Edition. McGill-Queen's University Press, 2016). [Page 232]. Reprint Edition. McGill-Queen's University Press, 2016.

Fanon, Frantz. *Black Skin, White Masks*. Translated by Charles Lam Markmann. New York: Grove Press, 1967.

Frankl, Viktor E. *Man's Search for Meaning*. New York: Beacon Press, 2006.

Goffman, Erving. *The Presentation of Self in Everyday Life*. New York: Doubleday, 1959.

Graeber, David. Debt: *The First 5,000 Years*. Brooklyn, NY: Melville House, 2011.

Haider, Asad. *Mistaken Identity: Race and Class in the Age of Trump*. London: Verso, 2018.

Harari, Yuval Noah. *Sapiens: A Brief History of Humankind*. Translated by Deri De Sola. New York: Harper, 2015.

Hayes, Steven C., Stefan G. Hofmann, and David H. Barlow, Eds. "Acceptance and Commitment Therapy: Model, Processes, and Outcomes." New York: Guilford Press, 2013.

Hooks, Bell. *Feminism Is for Everybody: Passionate Politics*. Cambridge, MA: South End Press, 2000.

James, William. *The Principles of Psychology*. Vol. 1. New York: Henry Holt and Company, 1890. Reprint, 1983.

Jung, Carl. "Aion: Researches into the Phenomenology of the Self." Translated by R. F. C. Hull. Princeton, NJ: Princeton University Press, 1959.

Kafka, Franz. *The Metamorphosis*. Translated by David Wyllie. New York: Dover Publications, 1996.

Kelly, Michael R., Ed. *Bergson and Phenomenology*. New York: Palgrave Macmillan, 2010.

Kerr, Daniel. "Judith Butler: Their Philosophy of Gender Explained." *The Conversation*. July 11, 2022. Https://Theconversation.Com/Judith-Butler-Their-Philosophy-of-Gender-Explained-192166.

Krishnamurti, J. *The Awakening of Intelligence*. New York: Harper & Row, 1973.

Kteily, Nour & Bruneau, Emile & Waytz, Adam & Cotterill, Sarah. (2015). "The Ascent of Man: A Theoretical and Empirical Case for Blatant Dehumanization. Journal of Personality and Social Psychology." 10.1037/T49381-000.

Kteily, Nour, Gordon Hodson, and Emile Bruneau. "They See Us As Less Than Human: Meta-Dehumanization Predicts Intergroup Conflict Via Reciprocal Dehumanization." *Journal of Personality and Social Psychology* 110 (2016): Https://Doi.Org/10.1037/Pspa0000044.

Landry, A. "Dehumanization Is Threatening Democracy." *SPSP*. Https://Www.Spsp.Org/News-Center/Blog/Landry-Dehumanization-Democracy-Threat. Retrieved April 3, 2022.

Landry, A. P., E. Ihm, S. Kwit, and J. W. Schooler. "Metadehumanization Erodes Democratic Norms During the 2020 Presidential Election." *Analyses of Social Issues and Public Policy* (2021): 1-13. Https://Doi.Org/10.1111/Asap.12253.

Lett, E., E. N. Asabor, T. Corbin, et al. "Impact of Socioeconomic Factors on Health Outcomes." *Journal of Epidemiology and Community Health*. Epub Ahead of Print January 15, 2021. Https://Doi.Org/10.1136/Jech-2020-215097.

Marcel, Gabriel. *The Mystery of Being*. Vol. 1. Translated by Kathleen Farrer. Chicago: Henry Regnery Company, 1951.

Martin, A. E. "Gender Relativism: How Context Shapes What Is Seen as Male and Female." *Journal of Experimental Psychology: General* 152, No. 2 (2023): 322–345. Https://Doi.Org/10.1037/Xge0001264.

McAdams, Dan P. *The Art and Science of Personality Development.* New York: Guilford Press, 2015.

McCrae, Robert R., and Paul T. Costa, Jr. "An Introduction to the Five-Factor Model and Its Applications." *Journal of Personality* 60, No. 2 (June 1992): 175–215. Https://Doi.Org/10.1111/j.1467-6494.1992. Tb00970.x.

Morrison, Toni. *The Bluest Eye.* New York: Holt, Rinehart and Winston, 1970.

Nietzsche, Friedrich. *Beyond Good and Evil.* Translated by Judith Norman. Cambridge: Cambridge University Press, 2002.

Pavetich, M., and S. Stathi. "Meta-Humanization Reduces Prejudice, Even Under High Intergroup Threat." *Journal of Personality and Social Psychology* 120, No. 3 (2021): 651–671. Https://Doi.Org/10.1037/ Pspi0000259.

Pettigrew, T. F., and L. R. Tropp. "A Meta-Analytic Test of Intergroup Contact Theory." *Journal of Personality and Social Psychology* 90, No. 5 (2006): 751–783. Https://Doi.Org/10.1037/0022-3514.90.5.751.

Pew Research Center. "Political Polarization in the American Public." Pew Research Center - U.S. Politics & Policy, April 9, 2021. Https://Www. Pewresearch.Org/Politics/2014/06/12/Political-Polarization-in-the-American-Public/. Retrieved April 3, 2022.

Popper, K. R., G. Soros, A. Ryan, and E. H. Gombrich. *The Open Society and Its Enemies: One-Volume Edition.* Princeton University Press, 2020.

Residential Schools. The Canadian Encyclopedia. Last Modified September 20, 2019. Https://Www.Thecanadianencyclopedia.ca/En/ Article/Residential-Schools.

Rosa, Jonathan. *Looking Like a Language, Sounding Like a Race.* Oxford: Oxford University Press, 2018.

Rosenberg, Noah A., Jonathan K. Pritchard, Jeffrey L. Weber, Hugh M. Cann, Kenneth K. Kidd, Leonid A. Zhivotovsky, and Marcus W. Feldman. "Genetic Structure of Human Populations." Science 298, No. 5602 (December 20, 2002): 2381–2385. Https://Doi.Org/10.1126/ Science.1078311.

Ryder, Richard D. *Animal Liberation*. 2nd Ed. Oxford: Oxford University
    Press, 2000.

Sartre, Jean-Paul. *Intentionality: A Fundamental Idea of Husserl's
    Phenomenology*. Translated by Joseph Fell. Journal of the British
    Society for Phenomenology 1 (1970): 4–5.

Sartre, Jean-Paul. *Morts sans Sépulture*. Paris: Gallimard, 1949.

Sartre, Jean-Paul. *No Exit*. Translated by Stuart Gilbert. New York: Vintage
    Books, 1989.

Sartre, Jean-Paul. *The Anti-Semite and the Jew*. Translated by George J.
    Becker. New York: Schocken Books, 1965.

Serano, Julia. *Whipping Girl: A Transsexual Woman on Sexism and the
    Scapegoating of Femininity*. Berkeley: Seal Press, 2007.

Singer, Peter. *Animal Liberation*. New York: Random House, 1990. First
    Published 1975.

Sokolowski, Robert. "Edmund Husserl." *Stanford Encyclopedia of
    Philosophy*. Last Modified November 23, 2020. Https://Plato.Stanford.
    Edu/Archives/Win2020/Entries/Husserl/.

Somer, M., and J. McCoy. "Transformations through Polarizations and
    Global Threats to Democracy." *The ANNALS of the American Academy
    of Political and Social Science* 681, No. 1 (2019): 8–22. Https://Doi.
    Org/10.1177/0002716218818058.

Stansfeld, S., and M. Marmot. "Psycho-Social Working Conditions and
    Health: A Longitudinal Study of Whitehall II." *Social Science &
    Medicine* 46, No. 5 (1998): 719–727. Https://Doi.Org/10.1016/S0277-
    9536(97)00243-8.

Stoltz, K., and M. Apodaca. "The Work Life Task: Adler's Influence on
    Career Counseling and Development." *Journal of Individual Psychology*
    73, No. 4 (2017).

Thompson, L. Stephen J., Ed. *Thirteen Theories of Human Nature*. 7th Ed.
    New York: McGraw-Hill Education, 2017.

Yuan, K. "The Impossibility of Centrism." *The Atlantic*, August 1, 2018.
    Https://Www.Theatlantic.Com/Membership/Archive/2018/08/the-
    Impossibility-of-Centrism/566570/. Retrieved April 3, 2022.

Part 2

Bateson, Gregory. "Social Conflict and Schismogenesis." *Man* 2, No. 3 (1967): 276–282. Https://Doi.Org/10.2307/2798253.

Han, Byung-Chul. *Psychopolitics: Neoliberalism and New Technologies of Power*. Translated by Erik M. Butler. London: Verso Books, 2017.

Illouz, Eva. *Emotional Capitalism: How Investment Banks and Private Equity Shareholders Have Transformed the Economy*. New York: Polity Press, 2007.

Kierkegaard, Søren. *The Concept of Anxiety*. Translated by Reidar Thomte and Albert B. Anderson. Princeton, NJ: Princeton University Press, 1980. Originally Published as Begrebet Angest (1844).

Latour, Bruno. *After Lockdown: A Mediation*. Cambridge: Polity Press, 2021.

Luhmann, Niklas. *The Differentiation of Society*. Translated by Stephen Holmes and Charles Larmore. New York: Columbia University Press, 1982.

Maté, Gabor, and Daniel Maté. *The Myth of Normal: Trauma, Illness, and Healing in a Toxic Culture*. New York: HarperCollins, 2022.

Moeller, Hans-Georg, and Paul J. D'Ambrosio. *Genuine Pretending: On the Philosophy of the Zhuangzi*. New York: Columbia University Press, 2018.

Moeller, Hans-Georg, and Peter J. D'Ambrosio. "Sincerity, Authenticity and Profilicity: Notes on the Problem, a Vocabulary and a History of Identity." *Philosophy & Social Criticism* 45, No. 5 (2019): 575–596. Https://Doi.Org/10.1177/0191453718799801.

Moeller, Hans-Georg, and Peter J. D'Ambrosio. "You and Your Profile: Notes on the Problem, a Vocabulary, and a History of Identity." *Philosophy & Social Criticism* 45, No. 5 (2019): 575–596. Https://Doi.Org/10.1177/0191453718799801.

Moeller, Hans-Georg. "Beyond Originality: The Birth of Profilicity from the Spirit of Postmodernity." *Kritike* 16, No. 2 (December 2022): 1–15. Https://Www.Kritike.Org/Journal/Issue_31/Moeller_december2022.Pdf.

Nietzsche, Friedrich. *Ecce Homo*. Translated by R.J. Hollingdale. London: Penguin Books, 2005.

Nietzsche, Friedrich. *The Gay Science*. Translated by Josefine Nauckhoff. Cambridge: Cambridge University Press, 2001. Originally Published as Die Fröhliche Wissenschaft (1882).

Palmer, Martin, Trans. *The Book of Chuang Tzu*. New York: Penguin Books, 1996.

Peterson, Jordan B. "On the Psychological and Social Significance of Identity." *Jordan B. Peterson*. August 25, 2023. Https://Www. Jordanbpeterson.Com/Blog-Posts/On-the-Psychological-and-Social-Significance-of-Identity/.

Selye, Hans. *The Stress of Life*. New York: McGraw-Hill, 1956.

Trilling, Lionel. *Sincerity and Authenticity*. Cambridge, MA: Harvard University Press, 1972.

Young, Jeffrey E., Janet S. Klosko, and Marjorie E. Weishaar. *Schema Therapy: A Practitioner's Guide*. 2nd Ed. New York: Guilford Press, 2014.

Part 3

Abelsen, Peter. "Schopenhauer and Buddhism." *Philosophy East and West*, Vol. 43, No. 2, 1993, Pp. 255–78. JSTOR, Https://Doi. Org/10.2307/1399616. Accessed 5 Aug. 2024.

Aristotle. *Nicomachean Ethics*. Translated by Terence Irwin. 2nd Ed. Indianapolis: Hackett Publishing Company, 1999.

Becker, Ernest. *The Denial of Death*. Reissue Edition. New York: Free Press, 2007.

Berlin, Isaiah. *Two Concepts of Liberty*. Oxford: Oxford University Press, 1958.

Cohen, S. Marc. "Aristotle's Psychology." *Stanford Encyclopedia of Philosophy*. Last Modified June 10, 2020. Https://Plato.Stanford.Edu/ Entries/Aristotle-Psychology/.

Csíkszentmihályi, Mihály. *Beyond Boredom and Anxiety*. San Francisco: Jossey-Bass, 2000.

Csíkszentmihályi, Mihály. *Flow: The Psychology of Optimal Experience*. Revised Edition. New York: HarperOne, 2008.

Csíkszentmihályi, Mihály. The Evolving Self: A Psychology for the Third Millennium. New York: HarperCollins, 1993.

Dewey, John. *How We Think: A Restatement of the Relation of Reflective Thinking to the Educative Process*. Boston: D.C. Heath & Co., 1910.

Fromm, Erich. *Escape from Freedom*. New York: Farrar & Rinehart, 1941.

Han, Byung-Chul. *The Palliative Society*. Translated by Eric B. Hansen. Cambridge: Polity Press, 2021.

Hesse, Hermann. *Siddhartha: Eine Indische Novel*. Zurich: S. Fischer Verlag, 1922.

Kasser, Tim, Steve Cohn, Allen D. Kanner, and Richard M. Ryan. 2007. "Some Costs of American Corporate Capitalism: A Psychological Exploration of Value and Goal Conflicts." *Psychological Inquiry* 18 (1): 1–22. Doi:10.1080/10478400701386579.

Kierkegaard, Søren. *The Concept of Anxiety*. Translated by Reidar Thomte and Albert B. Anderson. Princeton, NJ: Princeton University Press, 1980. Originally Published as Begrebet Angest (1844).

Marcia, James E. "Identity in Adolescence." *Handbook of Adolescent Psychology*, Edited by Judith Adelson, 159–187. New York: Wiley, 1980.

Marcia, James E. "The Ego Identity Status Approach to Ego Identity." *Ego Identity*, Edited by James Marcia, Anne Waterman, David Matteson, Susan Archer, and John Orlofsky, 3–21. New York: Springer Verlag, 1993.

Mill, John Stuart. *Collected Works of John Stuart Mill*. Edited by John M. Robson. Toronto: University of Toronto Press, 1963-1991.

Mineo, Liz. "Over Nearly 80 Years, Harvard Study Has Been Showing How to Live a Healthy and Happy Life." *Harvard Gazette*, April 11, 2017. Accessed March 1, 2023. Https://News.Harvard.Edu/Gazette/ Story/2017/04/over-Nearly-80-Years-Harvard-Study-Has-Been-Showing-How-to-Live-a-Healthy-and-Happy-Life/.

Nietzsche, Friedrich. *Beyond Good and Evil*. Translated by Judith Norman. Cambridge: Cambridge University Press, 2002.

Nietzsche, Friedrich. *Daybreak: Thoughts on the Prejudices of Morality*. Translated by R.J. Hollingdale. Cambridge: Cambridge University Press, 1982.

Pianciola, N. "The Collectivization Famine in Kazakhstan, 1931–1933." *Harvard Ukrainian Studies* 25, No. 3–4 (2001): 237–257.

Plath, Sylvia. *The Bell Jar*. New York: HarperCollins, 2005.

Ryan, Richard M., and Edward L. Deci, Eds. *The Oxford Handbook of Self-Determination Theory*. Oxford: Oxford University Press, 2017.

Ryan, Richard M., and Edward L. Deci. *Intrinsic Motivation and Self-Determination in Human Behavior*. New York: Plenum Press, 1985.

Sapolsky, Robert M. *Behave: The Biology of Humans at Our Best and Worst*. New York: Penguin Press, 2017.

Sapolsky, Robert M. *Determined: A Science of Life Without Free Will*. New York: Penguin Press, 2023.

Sartre, Jean-Paul. *Being and Nothingness: An Essay on Phenomenological Ontology*. Translated by Hazel Barnes. New York: Washington Square Press, 1992.

Schopenhauer, Arthur. *The World as Will and Representation*. Translated by Judith Norman. Cambridge: Cambridge University Press, 2010.

Trott, Michael. "Aristotle's Theory of Justice." *PhilArchive*. Accessed August 5, 2024. Https://Philarchive.Org/Archive/TROTHA-2#:~:text=2%2C%20Aristotle%20argues%20that%20a,Just%20(1253a14%%E2%80%9318).

Part 4

Camus, Albert. *L'Envers et l'Endroit*. Paris: Gallimard, 1937.

Camus, Albert. *The Myth of Sisyphus*. Translated by Justin O'Brien. New York: Alfred A. Knopf, 1955.

Camus, Albert. *Youthful Writings*. Translated by Richard Howard. New York: Alfred A. Knopf, 2003.

Csikszentmihalyi, Mihaly. *Finding Flow: The Psychology of Engagement with Everyday Life*. Illustrated Ed. New York: Basic Books, 1998.

De Beauvoir, Simone. *The Second Sex*. Translated by Constance Borde and Sheila Malovany-Chevallier. New York: Vintage Books, 2011.

Deleuze, Gilles, and Félix Guattari. *Anti-Oedipus: Capitalism and Schizophrenia*. Translated by Robert Hurley, Mark Seem, and Helen R. Lane. Minneapolis: University of Minnesota Press, 1983.

Deleuze, Gilles. *Difference and Repetition*. Translated by Paul Patton. London: Continuum, 2001.

Deleuze, Gilles. *Nietzsche and Philosophy*. Translated by Hugh Tomlinson. London: Continuum, 2002.

Frankfurt, Harry G. "Freedom of the Will and the Concept of a Person." *The Importance of What We Care About: Philosophical Essays*, 11–25. Cambridge: Cambridge University Press, 1988.

Fromm, Erich. *The Art of Loving*. New York: Harper & Row, 1956.

Funwa, Iluyomade Raphael. "The Self—A Thinking Thing or a Thinking Being? Insight from Shankarite and Cartesian Philosophies." *University of Toronto Press* 36, 3-4 (2013): 144-159 [Doi.Org/10.3138/ Uram.36.3-4.144].

Hanh, Thich Nhat. *Our Appointment with Life: A Call to the Buddha's Path*. Berkeley: Parallax Press, 2009.

Hayes, Stephen C., Kirk D. Strosahl, and Kelly G. Wilson. *Acceptance and Commitment Therapy: The Process and Practice of Mindful Change*. 2nd Ed. New York: Guilford Press, 2012.

Hollis, Roger. "bell hooks on Buddhism." *Tricycle: The Buddhist Review*. June 6, 2017. https://tricycle.org/magazine/bell-hooks-buddhism/.

Hooks, Bell. *All About Love: New Visions*. New York: HarperCollins, 2000.

Huta, V., and R. M. Ryan. "Pursuing Pleasure or Virtue: The Differential and Overlapping Well-Being Benefits of Hedonic and Eudaimonic Motives." *Journal of Happiness Studies* 11 (2010): 735–762. Https://Doi. Org/10.1007/S10902-009-9171-4.

Illouz, Eva. *Why Love Hurts: A Psychological Explanation*. Oxford: Oxford University Press, 2012.

Jaeggi, Rahel. *Alienation*. Translated by Frederick Neuhouser and Alan E. Smith. Edited by Frederick Neuhouser. New York: Columbia University Press, 2014.

Krishnamurti, J. *The Awakening of Intelligence*. New York: Harper & Row, 1973.

Loughrey, Dennis. 1998. "Second-Order Desire Accounts of Autonomy." *International Journal of Philosophical Studies* 6 (2): 211–29. Doi:10.1080/ 096725598342118.

Miller, Rachael. "Simone de Beauvoir's Authentic Love: A Project of Equals." *Aeon*. August 12, 2022. Https://Aeon.Co/Essays/Simone-de- Beauvoirs-Authentic-Love-Is-a-Project-of-Equals.

Nietzsche, Friedrich. *The Antichrist*. Translated by H. L. Mencken. New York: Alfred A. Knopf, 1921.

Nietzsche, Friedrich. *The Gay Science*. Translated by Josefine Nauckhoff. Edited by Keith Ansell-Pearson. Cambridge: Cambridge University Press, 2001.

Nietzsche, Friedrich. *The Will to Power*. Translated by Walter Kaufmann and R.J. Hollingdale. New York: Vintage Books, 1968.

Overmier, J. B., and M. E. P. Seligman. "Effects of Inescapable Shock upon Subsequent Escape and Avoidance Responding." *Journal of Comparative and Physiological Psychology* 63 (1967): 28–33.

Peterson, C., and M. E. P. Seligman. "The Learned Helplessness Model of Depression: Current Status of Theory and Research." *Handbook of Depression: Treatment, Assessment and Research*, Edited by E. E. Beckman and W. R. Leber, 914–939. Homewood, IL: Dorsey, 1985.

Roberts, Marc. "Capitalism, Psychiatry, and Schizophrenia: A Critical Introduction to Deleuze and Guattari's Anti-Oedipus." *Nursing Philosophy* 8 (2007): 114–127. Journal Compilation 2007 Blackwell Publishing Ltd.

Rosa, Hartmut. *Resonance: A Sociology of Our Relationship to the World*. Translated by James C. Wagber. Cambridge: Polity Press, 2019.

Schiermer, Bjørn. "Beyond the Echo Chamber: An Interview with Hartmut Rosa on Resonance and Alienation." *Krisis* (2022). https://archive.krisis.eu/beyond-the-echo-chamber-an-interview-with-hartmut-rosa-on-resonance-and-alienation/.

Stark, Hannah. 2012. "Deleuze and Love." *Angelaki* 17 (1): 99–113. Doi:10.1080/0969725X.2012.671669.

Stillwater Meditation and Practice Community. "Being Here." *Stillwater Meditation and Practice Community*. Accessed August 5, 2024. Https://Www.Stillwatermpc.Org/Dharma-Topics/Being-Here-7-2/.

Wallace, David Foster. *Infinite Jest*. New York: Little, Brown and Company, 1996.

Waltz, Thomas J., and Steven C. Hayes. "Acceptance and Commitment Therapy." *Cognitive and Behavioral Theories in Clinical Practice*, Edited by Nikolaos Kazantzis, Mark A. Reinecke, and Arthur Freeman, 155–156. New York: Guilford Press, 2010.

Wittgenstein, Ludwig. *Philosophical Investigations*. Translated by G.E.M. Anscombe. Oxford: Blackwell Publishing, 1953.

Zaretsky, Robert. *A Life Worth Living: Albert Camus and the Quest for Meaning*. Harvard University Press, 2013. Https://Doi.Org/10.2307/j.Ctt6wpp9f.

About the Author

Ben Thomas is a Canadian-born researcher and writer who is currently pursuing his PhD in Clinical Psychology at McGill University. He is also the creator of Sisyphus 55, a YouTube channel focused on philosophy, psychology, and literature, which has garnered over one million subscribers and more than seventy-five million views. Ben has previously published psychological research on *eudaemonia* and *the good life*. On his podcast, he has interviewed politicians, academic researchers, social media influencers, and cult survivors, exploring topics such as love, existentialism, politics, and identity. In his personal life, Ben is an avid traveller, having volunteered at a giant tortoise breeding centre in the Gálapagos Islands, hiked Torres del Paine in Patagonia, and worked at an after-school program for at-risk youth in Buenos Aires, Argentina. Ben is committed to understanding the human experience, on an individual and societal level, through community and creativity. You can check out his work on his YouTube channel (https://www.youtube.com/@Sisyphus55) or write him an email at sisyphus089@gmail.com.

Printed in Dunstable, United Kingdom